HOW TO
SEE YOURSELF
AS YOU
REALLY ARE

His Holiness the
Dalai Lama

HOW TO
SEE
YOURSELF
AS YOU
REALLY ARE

Translated and Edited by
Jeffrey Hopkins

RIDER

LONDON · SYDNEY · AUCKLAND · JOHANNESBURG

First published in 2006 in the United States by Atria Books.

This edition first published in 2007 in Great Britain by Rider Books,
an imprint of Ebury Publishing, Random House,
20 Vauxhall Bridge Road, London SW1V 2SA

Random House Australia (Pty) Limited
20 Alfred Street, Milsons Point, Sydney,
New South Wales 2061, Australia

Random House New Zealand Limited
18 Poland Road, Glenfield,
Auckland 10, New Zealand

Random House South Africa (Pty) Limited
Isle of Houghton, Corner Boundary Road & Carse O'Gowrie,
Houghton 2198, South Africa

Random House Publishers India Private Limited
301 World Trade Tower, Hotel Intercontinental Grand Complex,
Barakhamba Lane, New Delhi 110 001, India

The Random House Group Limited Reg. No. 954009

Papers used by Rider are natural, recyclable products made from wood
grown in sustainable forests.

Printed and bound in Great Britain by Mackays of Chatham plc, Kent

A CIP catalogue record for this book is available from the British Library

ISBN 978-1-84-604039-9

Contents

Contents

Contents

Foreword

This book by His Holiness the Dalai Lama stems from a basic Buddhist notion that love and insight work cooperatively to bring about enlightenment, like the two wings of a bird. The overarching theme is that self-knowledge is the key to personal development and positive relationships. The Dalai Lama shows us how, in the absence of true self-knowledge, we hurt ourselves through misguided, exaggerated notions of self, others, external events, and physical things. Even our senses deceive us, drawing us into attachment and negative actions that can only come back to haunt us in the future. The book details how to overcome these mistakes in order to live from a realistic knowledge of our healthy interdependence.

The first part of this book shows how to draw back the deceptive aspect of our experience like a curtain; other approaches, such as suppressing lust and hatred, may be helpful, but they do not address this root problem. By directing our attention to the false veneer that so bedazzles our senses and our thoughts, His Holiness sets the stage for discovering the reality behind appearances. Our tacit acceptance of things as they seem is called ignorance, which is not just a lack of knowledge about how people and things actually exist but an active mistaking of their fundamental nature. True self-knowledge involves exposing and facing misconceptions about ourselves. The aim here is to find out how we get ourselves into trouble, then learn how to intervene on the ground floor of our counterproductive ideas.

Buddhist psychology is known for its detailed descriptions of the mind's workings, and His Holiness uses these insights in a practical way by helping readers catch hold of these processes through their own experience. His central theme is that our skewed perceptions of body and mind lead to disastrous mistakes, ranging from lust at the one extreme to raging hatred at the other, so that we are consistently being led into trouble as if pulled by a ring in our nose. By developing insight into this process, we can free ourselves, and those around us, from these endless scenarios of pain.

This part provides step-by-step exercises to develop our ability to recognize the disparity between how we appear to ourselves and how we actually are. Once we have recognized our warped assumptions for what they are, the second part of the book shows how to undermine them. The tools used to accomplish this transformation are renowned Buddhist reflections for questioning appearances, which the Dalai Lama illustrates with his own experiences. His Holiness guides readers through a variety of practical exercises to help us break down the illusions we have superimposed over and beyond what actually exists, and learn how to act in the world from a more realistic framework. This calls for valuing the interdependence of all things and appreciating the latticework of our relationships for the meaningful contribution it makes to our lives.

The book's third part describes how to harness the power of meditative concentration with insight to achieve immersion in our own ultimate nature, which undermines our problems at their very foundation. The fourth and fifth parts discuss how people and things actually do exist, since they do not exist in the way we assume. The Dalai Lama draws readers into noticing how everything depends on thought—how thought itself organizes what we perceive. His goal is to develop in us a clear sense of what it means to exist without misconception. Then the final part of the book explains the way this profound state of being enhances love by revealing how unnecessary destructive emotions and suffering actually are. In this way self-knowledge is seen as the key to personal development and positive relationships. Once we know how to put insight in the service of love and love in the service of insight, we come to the book's appendix, an overview of the steps for achieving altruistic enlightenment.

This book itself is an illustration of Tibet's contribution to world culture, reminding us of the importance of maintaining a homeland for its preservation. The light shining through the Dalai Lama's teachings has its source in that culture, offering insights and practices that so many of us need in ours.

Jeffrey Hopkins, Ph.D.
Emeritus Professor of Tibetan Studies
University of Virginia

Introduction:
My Perspective

When we rise in the morning and listen to the news or read the newspaper, we are confronted with the same sad stories—violence, wars, and disasters. It is clear that even in modern times precious life is not safe: I cannot recall a single daily news program without a report of crime somewhere. There is so much bad news nowadays, such an awareness of fear and tension, that any sensitive and compassionate being must question the "progress" we have made in our modern world.

Ironically, the most serious problems emanate from industrially advanced societies, where unprecedented literacy only seems to have fostered restlessness and discontent. There is no doubt about our collective progress in many areas—especially science and technology—but somehow our advances in knowledge are not sufficient. Basic human problems remain. We have not succeeded in bringing about peace, or in reducing overall suffering.

This situation brings me to the conclusion that there may be something seriously wrong with the way we conduct our affairs, which, if not checked in time, could have disastrous consequences for the future of humanity. Science and technology have contributed immensely to the overall development of humankind, to our material comfort and well-being as well as to our understanding of the world we live in. But if we put too much emphasis on these endeavors, we are in danger of losing those aspects of human knowledge that contribute to the development of an honest and altruistic personality.

Science and technology cannot replace the age-old spiritual values that have been largely responsible for the true progress of world civilization as we know it today. No one can deny the material benefits of modern life, but we are still faced with suffering, fear, and tension—perhaps more now than ever before. So it is only sensible to try to strike a balance between material development on the one side and development of spiritual values on the other. In order to bring about a great change, we need to revive and strengthen our inner values.

I hope that you share my concern about the present worldwide moral crisis, and that you will join me in calling on all humanitarians and religious practitioners who share this concern to contribute to making our societies more compassionate, just, and equitable. I say this not as a Buddhist or even as a Tibetan but simply as a human being. I also do not speak as an expert on international politics (though I unavoidably comment on these matters) but as a part of the Buddhist tradition, which like the traditions of other great world religions, is founded on the bedrock of concern for all beings. From this perspective, I share with you the following personal beliefs:

1. That universal concern is essential to solving global problems
2. That love and compassion are the pillars of world peace
3. That all world religions seek to advance world peace, as do all humanitarians of whatever ideology
4. That each individual has a responsibility to shape institutions to serve the needs of the world.

Let us consider these one by one.

1. UNIVERSAL CONCERN IS ESSENTIAL TO SOLVING GLOBAL PROBLEMS

Of the many problems we face today, some are natural calamities that must be accepted and faced with equanimity. Others, however, are of our own making, created by misunderstanding, and these can be corrected. One such problem arises from the conflict of ideologies, political or religious, when people fight one another over their beliefs, losing sight of the basic humanity binding us together as a single human family. We must remember that these different religions, ideologies, and political systems of the world arose to help human beings achieve happiness. We must not lose sight of this fundamental goal. At no time should we place means above ends: we must always maintain the supremacy of compassion over ideology.

By far the greatest single danger facing all living beings on our planet is the threat of nuclear destruction. I need not elaborate on this danger, but I would like to appeal to the leaders of the nuclear powers who literally hold the future of the world in their hands, to the scientists and technicians who continue to create these awesome weapons of destruction, and to all people at large to exercise sanity and to disarm. We know that in the event of a nuclear war there will be no victors because there will be no survivors! Is it not frightening just to contemplate such inhuman and heartless destruction? And is it not logical that we should remove the potential cause for our own destruction once we recognize it? Often we cannot overcome a problem because we do not know its cause or if we understand it, we do not have the means or the time to remove it. This is not the case with the nuclear threat.

Whether they belong to a more evolved species, such as humans, or to simpler ones, such as animals, all beings seek peace, comfort, and security. Life is as dear to the mute animal as it is to any human being; even the simplest insect strives for protection from dangers that threaten its life. Just as each one of us wants to live and does not wish to die, so it is with all other creatures, though their power to effect this varies.

Broadly speaking, there are two types of happiness and suffering: mental and physical. Since I believe that mental suffering and happiness are more influential than their physical counterparts, I usually stress training the mind as a strategy to manage suffering and attain a more lasting state of happiness. Happiness is a combination of inner peace, economic viability, and above all, world peace. To achieve such goals, I feel it is necessary to develop a sense of universal responsibility, a deep concern for all, irrespective of creed, color, sex, nationality, or ethnicity.

The premise behind universal responsibility is the simple fact that we all want the same thing. Every being wants happiness and does not want suffering. If we do not respect this fact, there will be more and more suffering on this planet. If we adopt a self-centered approach to life and constantly try to use others for our own self-interest, we may gain temporary benefits, but in the long run both personal happiness and world peace will be completely out of the question.

In their quest for happiness, humans have used different methods, and all too often, these means have been aggressive and harsh. Behaving in ways utterly unbecoming to humanity, people commit terrible cruelties, inflicting suffering upon other living beings for the sake of selfish gains. In the end, such shortsighted actions bring nothing but suffering—to ourselves and to others. Being born a human being is a rare event in itself, and it is wise to use this opportunity as beneficially as possible. We must keep in mind that we all want the same thing, so that one person or group does not seek happiness or glory at the expense of others.

All this calls for a compassionate approach to global problems. Globalization means that the world is rapidly becoming smaller and more interdependent, because of technology and international trade. As a result, we need one another more than ever before. In ancient times problems were mostly family-size, so they could be addressed at the family level, but that situation has changed. Today one nation's problems can no longer be satisfactorily resolved by itself alone; too much depends on the interests, attitudes, and cooperation of other nations. A universal approach to world problems is the only sound basis for world peace. We are so closely interconnected that without a sense of universal responsibility, an understanding that we really are part of one big human family, we cannot hope to overcome the dangers to our very existence, let alone bring about peace and happiness.

What does this entail? Once we recognize that all beings cherish happiness and do not want suffering, it becomes both morally wrong and pragmatically unwise to pursue our own happiness oblivious to the feelings and aspirations of all other members of our own human family.

Considering others when pursuing our own happiness leads us to what I call "wise self-interest," which hopefully will transform itself into "compromised self-interest," or better still, "mutual interest." Some people think that cultivating compassion is good for others but not necessarily for themselves, but this is wrong. You are the one who benefits most directly since compassion immediately instills in you a sense of calm (nowadays medical researchers have shown in scientific studies that a calm mind is essential for good health), inner strength, and a deep confidence and satisfaction, whereas it is not certain that the object of your feeling of compassion will benefit. Love and compassion open our own inner life, reducing stress, distrust, and loneliness. I quite agree with a Western doctor who recently told me that those people who often use the words *I, my,* and *me* are at greater risk of having a heart attack. When, because of self-centeredness, your view is narrowed to yourself, even a small problem will seem unbearable.

Although increasing interdependence among nations might be expected to generate more cooperation, it is difficult to achieve a spirit of genuine cooperation as long as people remain indifferent to the feelings and happiness of others. When people are motivated mostly by greed and jealousy, it is not possible for them to live in harmony. A spiritual approach may not provide an overnight solution to all the political problems caused by our present self-centered approach, but in the long run it will address the very basis of the problems that we face today, removing them at the root.

The world is becoming smaller now, to the degree that all parts of the world are obviously part of yourself. Thus, destruction of your enemy is destruction of yourself. The very concept of war is outdated. If the twentieth century was the century of bloodshed, the twenty-first has to be the century of dialogue.

If humankind continues to approach its problems from the perspective of temporary expediency, future generations will face tremendous difficulties. Global population is increasing, and our resources are being rapidly depleted. Consider the ruinous effects of massive deforestation on the climate, the soil, and global ecology as a whole. We are facing calamity because, guided by expediency and selfish interests, and not thinking of the entire family of living beings, we are not taking into account the earth and the long-term needs of life itself. If we do not think about these issues now, future generations may not be able to cope with them.

2. LOVE AND COMPASSION AS THE PILLARS OF WORLD PEACE

According to Buddhist psychology, most of our troubles stem from attachment to things that we mistakenly see as permanent. Operating from that misconception, we see aggression and competitiveness as helpful in the pursuit of what we imagine and desire. But this only foments belligerence. Such misguided thinking has always been going on in the human mind, but our ability to act on it has become greater, now that we have machines and techniques of enormous power to gather and consume resources. In this way, greed and aggression, spurred on by our ignorance of things as they really are, release more of their poison into the world. If problems are resolved in a humane way, they simply end, whereas if one tries inhumane ways, further problems are added to the previous ones.

The humane antidote to these problems is love and compassion, which are the essential ingredients of world peace. We are social animals; the main factors keeping us together are love and compassion. When you have love and compassion for a very poor person, your feelings are based on altruism. By contrast, love toward your husband, wife, children, or a close friend is often mixed with attachment, and when your attachment changes, your kindness may disappear. Complete love is based not on attachment but on altruism, which is the most effective response to suffering.

Love and compassion are what we must strive to cultivate in ourselves, extending their present boundaries all the way to limitlessness. Undiscriminating, spontaneous, unlimited love and compassion are possible even toward someone who has done harm to you—your enemy. And their power is astonishing.

Buddhism teaches us to view all sentient beings as our dear mothers and to show our gratitude to our mothers by loving all sentient beings. One of the first actions we took in life was to suck milk from our mother's nipple, mother's milk being the very symbol of love and compassion. Scientists have documented through research on monkeys that offspring who are separated from their mothers for a prolonged period are more tense and harsh, lacking the capacity to express friendliness to others, whereas those brought up with their mothers are more playful, which implies happiness. According to the Buddhist outlook, we are born and reborn countless numbers of times, which means it is conceivable that each sentient being has been our parent at one time or another. In this way all beings share family ties. From the moment of our birth, we are under the care and kindness of our parents; later in life, when we face the suffering of disease and old age, we are again dependent on the kindness of others. If at the beginning and end of our lives we depend upon the kindness of others, why in the middle of our lives should we not act kindly toward them? It is the pragmatic choice.

Developing a kind heart, a feeling of closeness for all beings, does not require following a conventional religious practice. It is not only for those who believe in religion. It is for everyone, regardless of race, religion, or political affiliation. It is for all who consider themselves to be, above all, members of the human family, who can embrace this larger and longer perspective. The basic values of love and compassion are present in us from the time of our birth, whereas racial, ethnic, political, and theological perspectives come later. Violence does not accord with our basic human nature, which may lead you to wonder why all sorts of violence become news but compassionate acts seldom do. The reason is that violence is shocking and not in conformity with our basic human nature, whereas we take compassionate acts for granted because they are closer to our nature.

Since we all wish to gain happiness and avoid suffering,

and since a single person is relatively unimportant in relation to countless others, we can see that it is worthwhile to share our possessions with others. Happiness that is a by-product of loving and serving others is far superior to what we gain from serving only ourselves.

Our lives are in constant flux, which generates many predicaments. But when these are faced with a calm and clear mind supported by spiritual practice, they can all be successfully resolved. When our minds are clouded by hatred, selfishness, jealousy, and anger, we lose not only control but also our judgment. At those wild moments, anything can happen, including war. Although the practice of compassion and wisdom is useful to us all, it is especially valuable for those responsible for running national affairs, in whose hands lie the power and opportunity to create a framework for world peace.

3. ALL WORLD RELIGIONS SEEK TO ADVANCE WORLD PEACE

The principles I have mentioned are in accordance with the ethical teachings of all world religions. I maintain that Buddhism, Christianity, Confucianism, Hinduism, Islam, Jainism, Judaism, Sikhism, Taoism, and Zoroastrianism all hold up love as an ideal, seek to benefit humanity through spiritual practice, and strive to make their followers better people. All religions teach moral precepts for the advancement of mind, body, speech, and action: do not lie or steal or take others' lives, and so on. Unselfishness is the common foundation laid down by all great spiritual teachers. This is the basis for leading their followers away from harmful deeds caused by ignorance and toward the path of goodness.

All religions agree on the necessity to manage the undisciplined mind, which harbors selfishness and other sources of trouble, and to point the way to a spiritual state that is peaceful, disciplined, ethical, and wise. In this sense I believe all religions have essentially the same message. Of course, there is no end of argument when religious differences arise from dogma and cultural diversity. However, it is much better to implement in daily life the goodness taught by all religions than to argue about minor differences in approach.

There are many religions seeking to bring comfort and happiness to humanity, just as there are many treatments for a particular disease. All religions endeavor to help living beings avoid misery and find happiness. Although we may prefer one religious perspective to another, there is a much stronger case for unity, stemming from common desires of the human heart. Each religion works to lessen suffering and contribute to the world; conversion is not the point. I do not think about converting others to Buddhism or merely furthering the Buddhist cause. Instead, I try to think of how I as a Buddhist can contribute to the happiness of all living beings.

While I point out the fundamental parallels between various world religions, I do not advocate a new "world religion." All the different religions of the world are needed to enrich human experience and world civilization. Our human minds, with all their variety, need different approaches to peace and happiness. It is just like varieties of food. Certain people find Christianity more appealing; others prefer Buddhism because it does not advocate a creator—everything depends upon your own actions. We could make similar cases for other religions as well. The point is clear: humanity needs all the world's religions to suit varied ways of life, diverse spiritual needs, and inherited national traditions.

It is from this perspective that I welcome efforts being made in various parts of the world for better understanding among different religions. The need for this is particularly urgent. If all religions make the betterment of humanity their main concern, they can work together for world peace. Ecumenical understanding will bring about the cohesion necessary for all religions to work together. Although this is an important step, we must remember that there are no quick or easy ways to navigate the doctrinal differences among various faiths, nor can we hope to come up with a new universal belief that satisfies everyone. Each religion makes its own distinctive contributions, and each in its own way is suited to the orientation of a particular group of people. The world needs them all.

There are two primary tasks for religious practitioners concerned with world peace. First, we must promote better interfaith understanding to create a workable degree of unity among all religions, which we can achieve in part by respecting each other's beliefs and by emphasizing our common concern for human well-being. Second, we must bring about a viable consensus on basic spiritual values that touch every human heart. These two steps will enable us to act both individually and in concert to create the spiritual conditions necessary for world peace.

Despite systematic attempts to replace spiritual values with political ideology and commercialism, the vast majority of humanity continues to believe in one religion or another. The tenacity of faith, even in the face of repressive political regimes, clearly demonstrates the potency of religion. This spiritual energy is power that can be harnessed to bring about world peace. Religious leaders and humanitarians all over the world have a special role to play in this respect.

Whether we will be able to achieve world peace or not, we have no choice but to work toward that goal. If we allow love and compassion to be dominated by anger, we will sacrifice the best part of our human intelligence—wisdom, our ability to decide between right and wrong. Along with selfishness, anger is one of the most serious problems facing the world today.

4. EACH INDIVIDUAL HAS A RESPONSIBILITY TO SHAPE INSTITUTIONS

Anger plays a large role in current conflicts, such as those in the Middle East and Asia, as well as those between highly industrialized and economically undeveloped nations, and so forth. These conflicts arise from a failure to understand how much we have in common. Answers cannot be found in the development and use of greater military force, nor are they purely political or technological. The problems we face today cannot be blamed upon one person or cause but are the symptoms of our own past negligence. What is required is an emphasis on what we share, which is basically a spiritual approach.

Hatred and fighting cannot bring happiness to anyone, even to the winners of battles. Violence always produces misery, so it is essentially counterproductive. It is time for world leaders to learn to transcend differences of race, culture, and ideology in order to regard one another with appreciation of our common human situation. To do so would uplift individuals, communities, nations, and the world at large.

Mass media, including the Internet, can make a considerable contribution here by giving greater coverage to human interest items that reflect the ultimate oneness of humanity. I hope that all international organizations, especially the United Nations, will be more active and effective in serving humanity and promoting international understanding. It will indeed be tragic if a few powerful members misuse world bodies such as the UN for their one-sided interests. The UN must become the chief instrument of world peace; it is the only source of hope for small, oppressed nations and hence for the planet as a whole.

Within each nation, the individual ought to be given the right to achieve happiness, and among nations, there must be equal concern for the welfare of even the weakest nations. I am not suggesting that one system is better than another and all should adopt it. On the contrary, a variety of political systems and ideologies is desirable given the diverse dispositions within the human community. This variety enhances our prospects for happiness; therefore, each national community should be free to evolve its own political and socioeconomic system, based on the principle of self-determination.

By the same token, because all nations are more economically dependent upon one another than ever before, human understanding must go beyond national boundaries to embrace the international community at large. Indeed, unless we can create an atmosphere of genuine cooperation, in which threatened or actual use of force is replaced by heartfelt understanding, world problems will only increase. Not only is the gap between rich and poor morally wrong but as a practical matter it is a source of problems. If people in poorer countries are denied the happiness they desire and deserve, they will be dissatisfied and pose problems for the rich. If unwanted social, political, and cultural restrictions continue to be imposed upon unwilling people, the prospects for world peace grow dim. However, if we satisfy people at a heart-to-heart level, peace will surely ensue.

I realize the enormity of the task before us, but I see no alternative other than the one I am proposing, which is based on our common humanity. Nations have no choice but to be concerned about the welfare of others, not only because of the shared aspirations of all humanity but also because it is in the mutual and long-term interest of all concerned. We must also consider human benefit in the long run rather than just the short term.

In the past attempts have been made to create more just and equal societies. Institutions have been established with noble charters to combat antisocial forces. Unfortunately, such efforts have been undermined by selfishness and greed. Today we bear witness to the way ethics and noble principles are obscured by self-interest, particularly in the political sphere. Politics devoid of ethics does not further human welfare, and life without morality reduces humans to the level of beasts. This leads some of us to refrain from politics altogether, but politics is not axiomatically dirty. Rather, the misguided instruments of our political culture have distorted our high ideals and noble aspirations.

Morality, compassion, decency, and wisdom are the building blocks of all civilizations. These qualities must be cultivated in childhood and sustained through systematic moral education in a supportive social environment so that a more humane world may emerge. We cannot wait for the next generation to make this change; we ourselves must attempt a renewal of basic human values. Hope lies in future generations, but not unless we institute major change on a worldwide scale in our educational systems now. We need a revolution in commitment to universal values.

It is not enough to make noisy calls to halt moral degeneration; we must do something about it. Since present-day governments do not shoulder such "religious" responsibilities, humanitarians and religious leaders must strengthen existing civic, social, cultural, educational, and religious organizations to revive human and spiritual values. Where necessary, we must create new organizations to achieve these goals. Only in so doing can we hope to create a more stable basis for world peace. The seed of love and compassion is there in us intrinsically, but promoting and nurturing it have to be done through insight and education. To solve the problems humanity is facing, we need to organize meetings of scholars, educators, social workers, neuroscientists, physicians, and experts from all fields to discuss the positive and negative sides of what we have done thus far, as well as what needs to be introduced and what needs to be changed in our educational system. Proper environment plays a crucial role in the healthy growth of a child. All problems, including terrorism, can be overcome through education, particularly by introducing concern for all others at the preschool level.

Living in society, we must share the suffering of our fellow citizens and practice compassion and tolerance not only toward our loved ones but also toward our enemies. This is the test of our moral strength. We must set an example by our own practice. We must live by the same high standards of integrity we seek to convey to others. The ultimate purpose is to serve and benefit the world.

My intention in this book is to make a contribution, however small, to world peace by explaining Buddhist notions about finding the source of hurtful emotions, such as lust and hatred, within ourselves, and then describing Buddhist practices to undermine these painful influences and supplant them in the heart with insight and love.

Part I

THE NEED FOR INSIGHT

I

Laying the Ground for Insight to Grow

When starting to practice, be eager like a deer
trapped in a pen seeking to get out.
In the middle be like a farmer during harvest
not waiting for anything.
In the end be like a shepherd who has
brought the flock home.

—PALTRUL RINPOCHE'S *SACRED WORD*

What makes all this trouble in the world? Our own counterproductive emotions. Once they are generated, they harm us both superficially and deeply. These afflictive emotions accomplish nothing but trouble from beginning to end. If we tried to counteract each and every one individually, we would find ourselves in an endless struggle. So what is the root cause of afflictive emotions that we can address more fruitfully?

In the many scriptures of the Buddha, we find descriptions of practices to counter lust, such as meditating on what lies beneath the skin—flesh, bone, organs, blood, solid waste, and urine. These reflections do indeed temporarily suppress lust, but they do not accomplish the same for hatred. And the reverse is also true: those practices taught for the sake of undermining hatred, such as cultivating love, do not act as cures for lust. Like medicines used to counteract a specific illness, they do not treat other illnesses. However, because all counterproductive emotions are based on ignorance of the true nature of things, practices that teach us how to overcome that ignorance undercut all afflictive emotions. The antidote to ignorance addresses all troubles. This is the extraordinary gift of insight.

As preparation for developing insight into how you, other persons, and things actually exist, it is crucial to study spiritual teachings closely, thinking about them again and again. This is important because in order to generate a state that allows us to penetrate clear through to reality, we must first correct our mistaken ideas about existence.

IDENTIFYING IGNORANCE

To succeed at developing insight, first you need to identify ignorance. Ignorance in this context is not just a lack of knowledge—it is an active misapprehension of the nature of things. It mistakenly assumes that people and things exist in and of themselves, by way of their own nature. This is not an easy concept to grasp, but it is very important to identify this faulty perception, for it is the source of destructive emotions such as lust and hatred. In Buddhism we repeatedly speak of emptiness, but if you do not see how people mistakenly attribute to things their own inherent existence, it is impossible to understand emptiness. You have to recognize, at least in a rough way, what you are falsely superimposing on phenomena before you can understand the emptiness that exists in its stead. Understanding how you actually exist, who you really are without the overlay of false imagination, is the main topic of this book.

All of the Buddha's many teachings are aimed at attaining liberation from cyclic existence—with its endless movement from one life to another—and achieving omniscience. Ignorance is the root of everything that stands in the way of these attainments. Ignorance binds us to suffering; therefore ignorance has to be clearly identified. To do so we must consider how this false quality of inherent existence appears to the mind, how the mind assents to it, and how the mind bases so many ideas on this fundamental mistake.

Ignorance is not just other than knowledge, it is the contradiction of knowledge. Scientists tell us that the more closely we examine things the more likely we are to find empty space. Ignorance, by relying on appearances, superimposes onto persons and things a sense of concreteness that, in fact, is not there. Ignorance would have us believe that these phenomena exist in some fundamental way. Through ignorance what we see around us seems to exist independently, without depending on other factors for its existence, but this is not the case. By giving people and things around us this exaggerated status, we are drawn into all sorts of overblown and ultimately hurtful emotions.

Identifying this false appearance of things and acknowledging our tacit assent to this illusion are the first steps toward realizing that you and other beings, as well as all other objects, do not exist the way they appear to; they do not exist so concretely and autonomously. In the process of developing an accurate assessment of who you actually are, you need to appreciate the disparity between how you appear to your own mind and how you indeed exist. The same holds true for other people and all the other phenomena of the world.

Meditative Reflection

Consider:

1. All counterproductive emotions are based on and depend upon ignorance of the true nature of persons and things.

2. There are specific ways to suppress lust and hatred temporarily, but if we undermine the ignorance that misconceives the nature of ourselves, others, and all things, all destructive emotions are undermined.

3. Ignorance sees phenomena which actually do not exist in and of themselves—as existing independent of thought.

2

Discovering the Source
of Problems

Attracted by light and heat, a moth flies into a flame.
Stunned by the sounds of a guitar,
a deer stands unaware of a hunter.
Drawn by the scent of a flower, a bug is trapped inside.
Attached to taste, a fish rushes to a hook.
Pulled to mud, an elephant cannot escape.

—PALTRUL RINPOCHE'S *SACRED WORD*

Our senses contribute to our ignorance. To our faculties of seeing, hearing, smelling, tasting, and feeling, objects seem to exist in their own right. Presented with this distorted information, the mind assents to this exaggerated status of things. Buddhists call such a mind "ignorant" for accepting this false appearance instead of resisting it. The ignorant mind does not question appearances to determine if they are correct; it merely accepts that things are as they appear.

Next we become committed to the seeming truth of the concreteness of objects, thinking, "If this is not true, what could possibly be true!" As we do so, our ignorant misapprehension gets stronger. For instance, when we first encounter something or someone nice, we briefly take notice of the object of our attention, merely recognizing its presence. The mind at this point is pretty much neutral. But when circumstances cause us to pay more attention to the object, it appears to be attractive in a way that is integral to the object. When the mind adheres to the object this way—thinking that it exists as it appears—lust for the object and hatred for what interferes with getting it can set in.

When our own self is involved, we emphasize that connection: now it is "*my* body," "*my* stuff," "*my* friends," or "*my* car." We exaggerate the object's attractiveness, obscuring its faults and disadvantages, and become attached to it as helpful in acquiring pleasure, whereby we are forcibly led into lust, as if by a ring in our nose. We might also exaggerate the object's unattractiveness, making something minor into a big defect, ignoring its better qualities, and now we view the object as interfering with our pleasure, being led into hatred, again as if by a ring in our nose. Even if the object does not seem to be either agreeable or disagreeable but just an ordinary thing in the middle, ignorance continues to prevail, although in this case it does not generate desire or hatred. As the Indian scholar-yogi Nagarjuna says in his *Sixty Stanzas of Reasoning*:

> How could great poisonous afflictive emotions
> not arise
> In those whose minds are based on inherent
> existence?
> Even when an object is ordinary, their minds
> Are grasped by the snake of destructive
> emotions.

Cruder conceptions of "I" and "mine" evoke grosser destructive emotions, such as arrogance and belligerence, making trouble for yourself, your community, and even your nation. These misconceptions need to be identified by watching your own mind.

As the Indian thinker and yogi Dharmakirti says in his exposition of Buddhist thinking:

In one who exaggerates self
There is always adherence to "I."
Through that adherence there is attachment to
   pleasure.
Through attachment disadvantages are obscured
And advantages seen, whereby there is strong
   attachment,
And objects that are "mine" are taken up as means
   of achieving pleasure.
Hence, as long as there is attraction to self,
So long do you revolve in cyclic existence.

It is crucial to identify and recognize different thought processes. Some thoughts merely make us aware of an object, such as seeing a watch as just a watch without any afflictive emotions like lust. Other thoughts determine correctly that an object is good or bad but still do not introduce any afflictive emotions; these thoughts just recognize good as good and bad as bad. However, when the idea that objects inherently exist takes hold, fundamental ignorance has been introduced. As the mistaken assumption of inherent existence becomes stronger, lust or hatred become involved.

The turning point from mere awareness to misconception comes when ignorance exaggerates the status of the goodness or badness of the object so that it comes to be seen as *inherently* good or bad, *inherently* attractive or unattractive, *inherently* beautiful or ugly. Ignorantly misjudging this false appearance to be fact opens the way for lust, hatred, and myriad other counterproductive emotions. These destructive emotions, in turn, lead to actions based on lust and hatred. These actions establish karmic predispositions in the mind that drive the process of cyclic existence from life to life.

THE ROOT OF CYCLIC EXISTENCE

The process I just described is how we are ruined by our own ignorance and fixed to this round of suffering in life after life that we call "cyclic existence"; some levels of mind which we normally identify as correct are actually exaggerations of the status of persons and things that create trouble for ourselves and others. Ignorance keeps us from seeing the truth, the fact that people and other phenomena are subject to the laws of cause and effect but do not have essential being that is independent in and of themselves.

You need to identify this process as well as you can,

gradually developing greater and greater understanding of the sequence of events beginning with dispassionate observation and culminating in counterproductive emotions and actions. Without ignorance, counterproductive emotions are impossible; they cannot occur. Ignorance is their support. This is why Nagarjuna's student the Indian scholar-yogi Aryadeva says:

> Just as the capacity to feel is present throughout
>   the body,
> Ignorance dwells in all afflictive emotions.
> Therefore all afflictive emotions are overcome
> Through overcoming ignorance.

Meditative Reflection

Consider:

1. Does the attractiveness of an object seem to be integral to it?
2. Does the attractiveness of an object obscure its faults and disadvantages?
3. Does exaggeration of the pleasantness of certain objects lead to lust?

4. Does exaggeration of the unpleasantness of certain objects lead to hatred?

5. Notice how you:

   First perceive an object

   Then notice if the object is good or bad

   Then conclude that the object has its own independent basis for existing

   Then conclude that the object's goodness or badness exists inherently in the object

   Then generate lust or hatred according to your previous judgment.

3

Why Understanding the Truth Is Needed

Much of our planning is like waiting to swim
in a dry ravine.
Many of our activities are like housekeeping
in a dream.
Delirious with fever, one does not recognize the fever.

—PALTRUL RINPOCHE'S *SACRED WORD*

If you do not have insight into the way you yourself and all things actually are, you cannot recognize and get rid of the obstacles to liberation from cyclic existence and, even more important, the obstructions to helping others. Without insight you cannot address any problem at its root or remove the seeds that might produce it in the future.

To overcome the misconception that things and people exist as self-sufficient entities, independent of consciousness, it is essential to observe your own mind to discover how this mistake is being conceived, and how other destructive emotions arise with such ignorance as their support. Given that lust, hatred, pride, jealousy, and anger stem from exaggerating the importance of qualities such as beauty and ugliness, it is crucial to understand how persons and things actually exist, without exaggeration.

The only way to gain this understanding is internal. You need to give up the false beliefs you are superimposing on the way things really are; there is no external means of removing lust and hatred. If you are pierced by a thorn, you can remove it forever with a needle, but to get rid of an internal attitude, you must see clearly the mistaken beliefs on which it is based. This calls for using reason to explore the true nature of phenomena and then concentrate on what has been understood. This is the path leading to liberation and omniscience. As Dharmakirti says:

> Without losing belief in the object of an afflictive
>   emotion
> It cannot be abandoned.
> The abandonment of desire, hatred, and so forth,
> Which are related to misperceiving advantages and
>   disadvantages,

Is through not seeing those in objects,
Not through external ways.

When you see that all troublesome emotions—and indeed all problems—arise from a basic misunderstanding, you will want to get rid of such ignorance. The means to accomplish this is to reflect on reasoning that reveals the superimposition of a belief in inherent existence to be totally unfounded, and then to concentrate on the emptiness of inherent existence through meditation. As Chandrakirti, a follower of Nagarjuna and Aryadeva, said:

Seeing with their minds that all afflictive emotions
    and defects
Arise from viewing oneself as inherently existent
And knowing that the self is the object of this,
Yogis refute their own inherent existence.

Aryadeva similarly says that realization of selflessness is the way to stop cyclic existence:

When selflessness is seen in objects,
The seed of cyclic existence is destroyed.

When the roots of a tree are cut, all the branches, twigs, and leaves dry up. In the same way, all the problems of cyclic existence are undermined by removing the misunderstanding that is their cause.

The supreme scholar-practitioners of India—Nagarjuna, Aryadeva, Chandrakirti, and Dharmakirti—understood that the truth cannot be realized without seeing that we superimpose on people and things a status of solidity and permanence that actually is not there. The emptiness of that false superimposition must be understood, and to do this they analyzed phenomena through scripture and through reasoning.

HOW TO MAKE MEDITATION MEANINGFUL

It is crucial to understand this procedure, because if you do not meditate on the absence of the mistake that is the root of ruination, your meditation will not address the problem at all, no matter how profound you may think your meditation is. Although you might succeed in withdrawing your mind from disturbing objects, this does not constitute being absorbed in the truth. You have to actively realize that objects simply do not exist the way ignorance takes them to exist.

If someone is suffering from fright because she or he mistakenly believes that a snake is just outside the door, it would not help to point out that there is a tree on the other side of house; instead you need to show the person that in fact there is no snake outside the door. In the same way, you need to understand that the very objects you imagine to exist in and of themselves do not actually exist that way in order to get over the problems this misperception creates. Merely withdrawing your mind from thinking about anything or merely thinking about something else will not get to the root of the problem.

You have to put together that if objects really did exist in the way they seem to, the logical consequences would be impossible, and on this basis you can fully appreciate that phenomena do not exist this way. People and things may still seem to exist concretely and independently from their own side, but you will know that they do not. Gradually, this awareness will weaken your misconceptions and diminish the trouble they cause. Since accepting appearances as truth is the basic problem, the antidote is to come to realize the falsity of appearances through reasoning.

THREE WAYS OF SEEING OBJECTS

There are three modes of mental operation on an object:

1. Conceiving the object to inherently exist, which is what ignorance does
2. Conceiving the object to not inherently exist, which is what insight does
3. Conceiving the object without qualifying it with either inherent existence or an absence of inherent existence, as when just ordinarily seeing something, such as a house.

Even when you are not seeing an object as inherently existent, the way ignorance does, you are not necessarily seeing it as not inherently existent, the way insight does, since there are thoughts that do neither, which fall into the third category. This is why you need to delineate specifically those phenomena about which you are making this fundamental mistake. Just thinking about something else will not reverse ignorance. It would be like searching for a robber in town after the robber has gone to the forest.

When ignorance is overcome, you will have uprooted

the mistaken beliefs that superimpose on objects qualities such as beauty and ugliness beyond what they actually have. Then all other afflictive emotions—lust, hatred, jealousy, belligerence, and so on—that have ignorance as their root are overcome. When afflictive emotions are removed, they can no longer motivate your actions (karma). Then your powerless birth and rebirth in cyclic existence driven by predispositions established by your actions (the other aspect of karma) are overcome, and liberation is attained.

You need to contemplate this progression so that it is clear to you, and then unerringly seek the truth. When you fully understand how you enter into and disengage from the round of suffering, you will appreciate and value knowing the way persons and things actually are. If you do not come to understand that ruinous attitudes can be extinguished, the existence of liberation will not be clear to you. But when you understand that mistaken perspectives can indeed be removed, your intention to achieve liberation will strengthen. This is why insight is so important.

Meditative Reflection

Consider this:

1. Ignorance leads to exaggerating the importance of beauty, ugliness, and other qualities.
2. Exaggeration of these qualities leads to lust, hatred, jealousy, belligerence, and so on.
3. These destructive emotions lead to actions contaminated by misperception.
4. These actions (karma) lead to powerless birth and rebirth in cyclic existence and repeated entanglement in trouble.
5. Removing ignorance undermines our exaggeration of positive and negative qualities; this undercuts lust, hatred, jealousy, belligerence, and so on, putting an end to actions contaminated by misperception, thereby ceasing powerless birth and rebirth in cyclic existence.
6. Insight is the way out.

Part II

HOW TO UNDERMINE IGNORANCE

4

Feeling the Impact of
Interrelatedness

A six-inch line is short relative to an eight inch line.
An eight-inch line is short relative to a ten-inch line.
—TIBETAN SAYING

If the mistaken view that people and things exist independently is the cause of all other counterproductive views and emotions, then one of the principal means of overcoming this mistaken outlook is to reflect on the fact that all phenomena arise dependently. As Nagarjuna's *Precious Garland of Advice* says:

When there is long, there has to be short.
They do not exist through their own nature.

This relativity is why Buddhists say that all phenomena are dependent-arisings rather than independent-arisings.

Through reflecting on dependent-arising, you will lose the belief that things exist in and of themselves. Nagarjuna says:

> The apprehension of inherent existence is the cause
>   of all unhealthy views.
> Afflictive emotions are not produced without this
>   error.
> Therefore, when emptiness is thoroughly known,
> Unhealthy views and afflictive emotions are
>   thoroughly purified.
>
> Through what is emptiness known?
> It is known through seeing dependent-arising.
> Buddha, the supreme knower of reality, said
> What is dependently produced is not inherently
>   produced.

Nagarjuna's student Aryadeva similarly says that understanding dependent-arising is crucial for overcoming ignorance:

> All afflictive emotions are overcome
> Through overcoming ignorance.

When dependent-arising is seen,
Ignorance does not arise.

Dependent-arising refers to the fact that all impermanent phenomena—whether physical, mental, or otherwise—come into existence dependent upon certain causes and conditions. Whatever arises dependent upon certain causes and conditions is not operating exclusively under its own power.

Meditative Reflection

1. Bring to mind an impermanent phenomenon, such as a house.
2. Consider its coming into being in dependence upon specific causes: lumber, carpenters, and so forth.
3. See if this dependence conflicts with the house's appearing as if it exists in its own right.

DEPENDENT-ARISING AND REALISM

The theory of dependent-arising can be applied everywhere. One benefit of applying this theory is that viewing a situation this way gives you a more holistic picture, since whatever the situation is—good or bad—it depends on causes and conditions. An event is not under its own power but depends on many present causes and conditions as well as many past causes and conditions. Otherwise, it could not come into being.

When you think from this viewpoint, you can see much more of the whole picture, and from this wider perspective, you can see the reality of the situation, its interdependence. With the help of this relational outlook, the action that you take will be realistic. In international politics, for example, without such an outlook a leader might see a problem as created by a single person, who then becomes an easy target. But that is not realistic; the problem is much wider. Violence produces a chain reaction. Without a broader perspective, even if the motivation is sincere, any attempt to handle the situation becomes unrealistic; the actions taken will not be well founded because of the lack of a holistic picture, of understanding the web of causes and conditions involved.

In the field of medicine also, it is not sufficient to concentrate just on one specialty. The whole body needs to be considered. In Tibetan medicine, the diagnostic approach is more holistic, taking into consideration interactive systems. Similarly, in economics, if you just go after profit, you end up with corruption. Look at the increasing corruption in many countries. By considering all commercial actions to be morally neutral, we turn a blind eye to exploitation. When, as they say in China, "It doesn't make any difference whether a cat is black or white," the result is that a lot of black cats—morally bankrupt people—are creating a lot of problems!

Failure to look at the whole picture means realism is lost. The attitude that money alone is sufficient leads to unforeseen consequences. Money is certainly necessary; for instance, if you thought that religious retreat in meditation alone was sufficient, you would not have anything to eat. Many factors have to be considered. With awareness of the fuller picture, your outlook becomes reasonable, and your actions become practical, and in this way favorable results can be achieved.

The chief drawback of afflictive emotions is that they obscure reality. As Nagarjuna says:

> When afflictive emotions and their actions cease,
>   there is liberation.
> Afflictive emotions arise from false conceptions.

False conceptions here are exaggerated modes of thought that do not accord with the facts. Even if an object—an event, a person, or any other phenomenon—has a slightly favorable aspect, once the object is mistakenly seen as existing totally from its own side, true and real, mental projection exaggerates its goodness beyond what it actually is, resulting in lust. The same happens with anger and hatred; this time a negative factor is exaggerated, making the object seem to be a hundred percent negative, the result being deep disturbance. Recently, a psychotherapist told me that when we generate anger, ninety percent of the ugliness of the object of our anger is due to our own exaggeration. This is very much in conformity with the Buddhist idea of how afflictive emotions arise.

At the point when anger and lust are generated, reality is not seen; rather, an unreal mental projection of extreme badness or extreme goodness is seen, evoking twisted, unrealistic actions. All of this can be avoided by seeing the fuller picture revealed by paying attention to the dependent-arising of phenomena, the nexus of causes and conditions from which they arise and in which they exist.

Looked at this way, the disadvantages of afflictive emotions are obvious. If you want to be able to perceive the actual situation, you have to quit voluntarily submitting to afflictive emotions, because in each and every field, they obstruct perception of the facts. Viewed from the perspective of lust or anger, for example, the facts are always obscured.

Love and compassion also involve strong feelings that can even make you cry with empathy, but they are induced not by exaggeration but by valid cognition of the plight of sentient beings, and the appropriateness of being concerned for their well-being. These feelings rely on insight into how beings suffer in the round of rebirth called "cyclic existence," and the depth of these feelings is enhanced through insight into impermanence and emptiness, as will be discussed in Chapters 22 and 23. Though it is possible for love and compassion to be influenced by afflictive emotions, true love and compassion are unbiased and devoid of exaggeration, because they are founded on valid cognition of your relationship to others. The perspective of dependent-arising is supremely helpful in making sure that you appreciate the wider picture.

DEPENDENCE UPON PARTS

Dependent-arising also refers to the fact that all phenomena—impermanent and permanent—exist in dependence upon their own parts. Everything has parts. A pot, for instance, exists in dependence upon its parts, whether we consider coarse parts, such as the lid, handle, or opening, or subtle parts, such as molecules. Without its essential parts, a pot simply cannot be; it does not exist in the concrete, independent way that it seems to.

What about the atomic particles that are the building blocks of larger objects? Could they be partless? This too is impossible, since if a particle did not have spatial extent, it could not combine with other particles to form a larger object. Particle physicists believe that even the tiniest particle can be broken down into smaller parts if we can create tools powerful enough to do so, but even if they found a physically unbreakable entity, it would still have spatial extent and thus parts; otherwise it could not combine with other such entities to form anything larger.

Meditative Reflection

1. Bring to mind an impermanent phenomenon, such as a book.
2. Consider its coming into being in dependence upon its parts—its pages and cover.
3. See if its dependence upon its parts conflicts with its appearing as if it exists in its own right.

EXAMINING CONSCIOUSNESS

The consciousness involved in looking at a blue vase does not have spatial parts because it is not physical, but it exists as a continuum of moments. Consciousness looking at a blue vase has earlier and later moments in its continuum, and these are parts of a stream of consciousness—no matter how short.

Then consider the briefest moments in a continuum. If even the briefest of moments did not have a beginning, middle, and end, it could not join with other brief moments to become a continuum; it would be equally close to an earlier moment and to a later moment, in which case there would be no continuum at all.

As Nagarjuna says:

Just as a moment has an end, so it must have
A beginning and a middle.
Also the beginning, middle, and end
Are to be analyzed like a moment.

Meditative Reflection

1. Consider consciousness paying attention to a blue vase.
2. Reflect on its coming into being in dependence upon its parts—the several moments that constitute its continuum.
3. See if its dependence upon its parts conflicts with its appearing as if it exists in its own right.

EXAMINING SPACE

Even space has parts, such as the space associated with particular directions, such as space in the east and space in the west, or particular objects.

Meditative Reflection

1. Consider space in general.
2. Reflect on its coming into being in dependence upon its parts—north, south, east, and west.
3. See if its dependence upon its parts conflicts with its appearing as if it exists in its own right.

Also:

1. Consider the space of a cup.
2. Reflect on its coming into being in dependence upon its parts—the top half and the bottom half of the cup.
3. See if its dependence upon its parts conflicts with its appearing as if it exists in its own right.

5

Appreciating the Reasoning
of Dependent-Arising

Because there are no phenomena
That are not dependent-arisings,
There are no phenomena that are not
Empty of inherent existence.

—NAGARJUNA'S *FUNDAMENTAL TREATISE*
ON THE MIDDLE CALLED "WISDOM"

As explained in the previous chapter, all phenomena, whether impermanent or permanent, have parts. The parts and the whole depend on other, but they *seem* to have their own entities. If the whole and its parts existed the way they appear to you, you should be able to point out a whole that is separate from its parts. But you cannot.

There is a conflict between the way the whole and its

parts appear and the way they actually exist, but this does not mean that there are no wholes, because if wholes did not exist, you could not speak of something as being a part of anything. The conclusion must be that there are wholes but their existence is set up in dependence upon their parts—they do not exist independently. As Nagarjuna's *Fundamental Treatise on the Middle Called "Wisdom"* says:

> That which arises dependently
> Is not one with that on which it depends
> And is also not inherently other than it.
> Hence, it is not nothing and not inherently
> existent.

HOW THE REASONING OF DEPENDENT-ARISING WORKS

Dependent or independent: there is no other choice. When something is one, it is definitely not the other. Because dependent and independent are a dichotomy, when you see that something cannot be independent, or functioning under its own power, there is no other option but to see that it is dependent. Being dependent, it is empty of being under its own power. Look at it this way:

> A table depends for its existence on its parts, so we call the collection of its parts the basis upon which it is set up. When we search analytically to try to find this table that appears to our minds as if it exists independently, we must look for it within this basis—the legs, the top, and so forth. But nothing from within the parts is such a table. Thus, these things that are not a table become a table in dependence upon thought; a table does not exist in its own right.

From this viewpoint, a table is something that arises, or exists, dependently. It depends on certain causes; it depends upon its parts; and it depends upon thought. These are the three modes of dependent-arising. Of these, one of the more important factors is the thought that designates an object.

Existing in dependence upon conceptuality is the most subtle meaning of *dependent-arising*. (Nowadays, physicists are discovering that phenomena do not exist objectively in and of themselves but exist in the context of involvement with an observer.) For example, the Dalai Lama's "I" must be within this area where my body is; there is no other place it could possibly be found. This is clear. But when you investigate in this area, you cannot find an "I" that has its own substance. Nevertheless, the Dalai Lama is a man, a monk, a Tibetan, who can speak, drink, eat, and sleep. This is sufficient proof that he exists, even though he cannot be found.

This means that there is nothing to be found that is the "I," but this fact does not imply that the "I" does not exist. How could it? That would be silly. The "I" definitely does exist, but when it exists yet cannot be found, we have to say that it arises in dependence upon thought. It cannot be posited any other way.

EMPTINESS DOES NOT MEAN NOTHINGNESS

There is no question that persons and things exist; the question is how, or in what manner, they exist. When we consider a flower, for instance, and think, "This flower has a nice shape, nice color, and nice texture," it seems as if there is something concrete that possesses these qualities of shape, color, and texture. When we look into these qualities, as well as the parts of the flower, they seem to be qualities or parts *of the flower,* such as the color of the flower, the shape of the flower, the stem of the flower, and the petals of the flower—as if there is a flower that possesses these qualities or parts.

However, if the flower really exists the way it appears, we should be able to come up with something separate from all of these qualities and parts that is the flower. But we cannot. Such a flower is not found upon analysis, or through other scientific tools, even though previously it seemed so substantial, so findable. Because a flower has effects, it certainly exists, but when we search to find a flower existing in accordance with our ideas about it, that is not at all findable.

Something that truly exists from its own side should become more and more obvious when analyzed—it should be clearly found. But the opposite is the case. Nevertheless, this does not mean that it does not exist, for it is effective—it creates effects. The fact that it is not found under analysis just indicates that it does not exist the way it appears to our senses and to our thoughts—that is, so concretely established within itself.

If not finding objects when they are analyzed meant

that they did not exist, there would be no sentient beings, no Bodhisattvas, no Buddhas, nothing pure, and nothing impure. There would be no need for liberation; there would be no reason to meditate on emptiness. However, it is obvious that persons and things help and harm, that pleasure and pain exist, that we can free ourselves from pain and gain happiness. It would be foolish to deny the existence of persons and things when we are obviously affected by them. The idea that persons and things do not exist is a denial of the obvious; it is foolish.

The Indian scholar-yogi Nagarjuna demonstrates that phenomena are empty of inherent existence by the fact that they are dependent-arisings. This itself is a clear sign that the view that phenomena do not inherently exist is not nihilistic. He does not give as the reason why phenomena are empty that they are unable to function; instead, he calls attention to the fact that they arise dependent on causes and conditions.

Meditative Reflection

Consider:

1. Dependent and independent are a dichotomy. Anything that exists is either the one or the other.

2. When something is dependent, it must be empty of being under its own power.

3. Nowhere in the parts of the body and mind that form the basis for the "I" can we find the "I." Therefore, the "I" is established not under its own power but through the force of other conditions—its causes, its parts, and thought.

6

Seeing the Interdependence
of Phenomena

Realizing the doctrine of dependent-arising,
The wise do not at all partake of extreme views.
—BUDDHA

Because phenomena *seem*, even to our senses, to exist
from their own side even though they do not, we mistakenly accept the view that phenomena exist more substantially than they actually do. In this way we are drawn into
afflictive emotions, creating the seeds of our own ruin. We
need to undo these problems by reflecting, again and
again, on the dependent nature of everything.

THE IMPACT OF DEPENDENT-ARISING

All phenomena—helpful and harmful, cause and effect,
this and that—arise and are established in reliance upon

other factors. As Nagarjuna says in his *Precious Garland of Advice:*

> When this is, that arises,
> Like short when there is long.
> Due to the production of this, that is produced,
> Like light from the production of a flame.

In this context of dependence, help and harm arise, impermanent phenomena can function (and are not just figments of the imagination), and karma—actions and their effects—is feasible. You are feasible, and I am feasible; we are not just mental creations. By understanding this, you are free from what Buddhists call "the extreme of nihilism," drawing the mistaken conclusion that just because a phenomenon cannot be found to exist independently it does not at all exist. As Nagarjuna says:

> Having thus seen that effects arise
> From causes, one asserts what appears
> In the conventions of the world
> And does not accept nihilism.

These two extremes—the exaggerated notion that phenomena exist under their own power, and the denial of cause and effect—are like chasms into which our minds can fall, creating damaging perspectives that either exaggerate the status of objects beyond their actual nature or deny the very existence of cause and effect. Falling into the chasm of exaggeration, we are drawn into satisfying a conception of ourselves that exceeds how we actually are—an impossible feat. Or, falling into the chasm of denial, we lose sight of the value of morality and are drawn into ugly actions that undermine our own future.

To be able to balance dependent-arising and emptiness, we need to differentiate between inherent existence and mere existence. It is also crucial to recognize the difference between the absence of inherent existence and utter nonexistence. This is why when the great Buddhist sages in India taught the doctrine of emptiness, they did not use the argument that phenomena are empty of the capacity to perform functions. Rather, they said that phenomena are empty of inherent existence because they are dependent-arisings. When emptiness is understood this way, both extremes are avoided. The exaggerated notion that phenomena exist from their own side is avoided through realizing emptiness, and the denial of the existence of functionality is avoided through understanding that phenomena are dependent-arisings and therefore not utterly nonexistent.

As Chandrakirti says:

This reasoning of dependent-arising
Cuts through all the nets of bad views.

Dependent-arising is the route for steering clear of the two chasms of mistaken outlooks and their attendant pains.

INEXPRESSIBILITY OF THE TRUTH

Once there was a fledgling scholar in a monastic college in Lhasa who was having a hard time debating, being unable to give a good response to a challenge. So he announced, to the amusement of all, that he knew all the answers but was having trouble expressing them in words. Maybe we—not knowing emptiness well—could just repeat the statement in our Buddhist scriptures that the perfection of wisdom is inconceivable and inexpressible and try to look profound! However, this statement means that the realization of emptiness *as it is directly experienced in nondu-alistic meditation* cannot be expressed in words; it does not mean that emptiness cannot be reflected and meditated upon.

When we say, hear, or think about terms such as *emptiness* or *ultimate truth,* they appear to us in separate subject and object—the consciousness on one side and emptiness on the other side—whereas in profound meditation, subject and object have one taste; emptiness and the consciousness perceiving it are like water put in water, undifferentiable.

SIMILARITY WITH ILLUSIONS

Using the tool of analysis, you cannot find a being that transmigrates from one lifetime to another, but this does not mean that rebirth does not in any way exist. Despite the fact that agent, action, and object cannot withstand analysis to stand independently, healthy and unhealthy actions leave their imprints in the mind, and these come to fruition either in this lifetime or in a future one.

If we investigate a person with this reasoning who appears in a dream and an actual person seen when we are awake, no self-instituting entity can be found for either of them. They are equally unfindable under such analysis, but this does not mean that there are no actual people or that a dream-person is an actual person. This would contradict valid perceptions. The fact that people and other objects are not findable under analysis means not that they do not exist but that they do not exist by way of their own power; they exist due to other factors. In this way, being empty of being under its own power comes to mean depending on others.

Meditative Reflection

Consider:

1. Inherent existence never did, never does, and never will exist.
2. However, we imagine that it does exist and thereby are drawn into distressing emotions.
3. The belief that phenomena inherently exist is an extreme of exaggeration, a frightful chasm.
4. The belief that impermanent phenomena cannot perform functions, or act as cause and effect, is an extreme form of denial, another frightful chasm.
5. The realization that all phenomena are empty of in-

herent existence because of being dependent-arisings avoids both extremes. Realizing that phenomena are dependent-arisings avoids the extreme of dangerous denial; realizing that they are empty of inherent existence avoids the extreme of dangerous exaggeration.

7

Valuing Dependent-Arising and Emptiness

Reliance on actions and their fruits
Within knowing this emptiness of phenomena
Is more wonderful than even the wonderful,
More fantastic than even the fantastic.

—NAGARJUNA'S *ESSAY ON THE MIND OF ENLIGHTENMENT*

Reflecting on how an object is a dependent-arising—arising dependent on causes and conditions, dependent upon its parts, and dependent on thought—greatly helps to overcome the sense that it exists in and of itself. However, if you do not figure out exactly what phenomena are empty of—what is being negated—then at the end of this analysis you will feel that the object does not exist at all.

This experience will cause phenomena to seem ephemeral, like insubstantial drawings, next to nothing. This mistake comes from not distinguishing between the absence of *inherent* existence and nonexistence. Failure to distinguish these makes it impossible to appreciate the dependent-arising of phenomena, whereas it is crucial to understand that emptiness means dependent-arising, and dependent-arising means emptiness.

FEASIBILITY OF CAUSE AND EFFECT

We need to be able to comprehend the dependent-arising of all agents, actions, and objects as a negation of their inherent existence and to see that cause and effect definitely exist. Indeed, an object is proved to be empty of inherent existence by reason of the fact that it is a dependent-arising, so dependently arisen dynamics, such as cause and effect, are totally viable. Emptiness is not an utter void that denies the existence of all phenomena but is an emptiness of inherent existence. Phenomena are empty of this status, they are not empty of themselves; a table is empty of inherent existence, it is not empty of being a table. Hence, due to emptiness—due to the lack of inherent existence—agent, action, and object are possible.

In this way, the fact of emptiness means that the object must exist, but it exists differently from what you imagined. After you have gotten a sense of emptiness, it is not sufficient just to claim that phenomena must exist but not have a clear sense of *how* they exist. You need to know from the depths of your being that understanding dependent-arising promotes understanding emptiness, and understanding emptiness promotes understanding dependent-arising.

REASONING FROM EMPTINESS TO DEPENDENT-ARISING

To me it seems easier to understand emptiness by reason of the fact that persons and things are dependent-arisings than it is to understand that an object has to be a dependent-arising due to the fact that it is empty of inherent existence. But here are my thoughts.

Within falsity, contradictions are completely feasible; for instance, a youthful person suddenly ages, or someone who is ignorant gradually turns into a scholar knowing much. In a world of inherently established fixed entities, such radical change would not be feasible. If a tree were truly, fundamentally as it is in summer, with features like leaves and fruit, then circumstances could not affect it and cause it to lose these features in winter. If its beauty was self-instituted, it could not turn ugly due to circumstance.

What is false can be all sorts of things, whereas what is true must be just as it is. When someone's word is not reliable, we say it is false. The fact that phenomena have a nature of falsity is what allows so much change, turning from good to bad and bad to good, developing and declining. Because persons and things are devoid of the trueness of being self-instituting, they are affected by conditions and are capable of transformation. Because youth is not an abiding truth, it can turn into old age.

Because phenomena are false in this sense, they are ready to immediately change: areas fill with people and then lose population; countries at peace start fighting wars; nations form and disappear. Good and bad, growth and decay, cyclic existence and nirvana, this way and that way: change happens in so many ways. The fact that people and phenomena change indicates that they actually do not have their own individual status just as they are; they are not able to set themselves up. Because they are foundationless, they can transform.

This is how cause and effect are feasible within an emptiness of inherent existence. If phenomena did exist in their own right, they could not depend on other factors. Without dependence on others, cause and effect are impossible. With cause and effect, unfavorable effects, such as pain, can be avoided by abandoning certain causes, like jealousy, and favorable effects, such as happiness, can be achieved by training in other causes, such as taking joy in others' success.

MUTUALLY SUPPORTIVE REALIZATION

Remember, it is preferable to set aside the doctrine of emptiness for the time being if it interferes with understanding cause and effect. Realization of emptiness must include the cause and effect of actions. If you think that because phenomena are empty there could not be any good or bad, you are making it harder to realize the import of emptiness. You need to value cause and effect.

Special Objects of Meditation

Sometimes it is helpful to take a person you hold in high regard as the object of this type of analysis—for instance, your own revered teacher or spiritual leader. In the light of those moments when you especially value your teacher, you will not fall into denying cause and effect, since you cannot deny that person's impact.

Emptiness is extremely important, because if you thoroughly understand it, you can be liberated from the cycle of destructive emotions, and through not understanding it you will be led, as if by the nose, into destructive emotions that induce lifetime after lifetime of suffering in cyclic existence. Nevertheless, when you consider that the emptiness of yourself depends on yourself or that the emptiness of a car depends on the car, that substratum of which emptiness is a quality seems almost more important than emptiness itself.

In this way, if you sometimes put emphasis on the appearance that is empty of inherent existence and at other times put emphasis on its emptiness of inherent existence, moving from the one to the other rather than just concentrating on emptiness, it can be helpful. Such alternating reflection helps ascertain both dependent-arising and emptiness, showing that emptiness is not off by itself, not isolated, but the very nature of phenomena. As the *Heart Sutra* says, "Form is emptiness; emptiness is form."

A form's natural lack of inherent existence itself is emptiness; emptiness is not something extra, like a hat on top of the head. Emptiness is the nature, the final character, of form itself. The Tibetan sage Tsongkhapa quotes a passage from the *Kashyapa Chapter* in the *Pile of Jewels Sutra*. "Emptiness does not make phenomena empty; phenomena themselves are empty." When I was in Ladakh a year or so ago, I found a similar passage in the *Twenty-five-Thousand-Stanza Perfection of Wisdom Sutra*: "Form is not made empty by emptiness; form itself is emptiness." I was stimulated to reflect on this profound statement, and I would like to share with you what I found. It is a bit complicated, so please bear with me.

First of all, it is undeniable that objects appear to exist from their own side, and even within Buddhism, most schools accept this appearance of things, saying that if objects, such as tables, chairs, and bodies, did not exist in their own right, there would be no way to posit that they exist. They say that a visual consciousness apprehending a table, for example, is valid in terms of its appearing to be objectively established, and according to those systems, there is no way that a consciousness could be both valid and mistaken. However, according to the system of the Middle Way School following Chandrakirti, called the Consequence School, which we hold to be the most profound depiction of how phenomena exist and how they are perceived, phenomena such as tables, chairs, and bodies just plain do not exist in their own right; visual consciousness is mistaken about how objects appear as if established in and of themselves, but that same consciousness is valid with respect to the presence of the objects. In this way, a consciousness can be both valid and mistaken at the same time—valid with respect to the presence of the object and its existence but mistaken in that the object seems to have its own independent status.

Chandrakirti posits that objects appear to exist from their own side due to a mistaken framework of ordinary perception. In fact, nothing is established from its own side. In this way, form itself *is* empty; it is not made empty by emptiness. What is it that is empty? The form itself. The table itself. The body itself. In the same way, all phenomena are empty of their own inherent existence. Emptiness is not something made up by the mind; this is how things have been from the start. Appearance and emptiness are one entity, and cannot be differentiated into separate entities.

Meditative Reflection

Consider:

1. Because persons and things are dependent-arisings, they are empty of inherent existence. Being dependent, they are not self-instituting.

2. Because persons and things are empty of inherent existence, they must be dependent-arisings. If phenomena did exist in their own right, they could not depend on other factors, either causes, their own parts, or thought. Since phenomena are not able to set themselves up, they can transform.

3. These two realizations should work together, the one furthering the other.

Enriching Practice

Understanding the reasoning of dependent-arising will deepen your analysis that the "I" and other things are not the same as or separate from the bases on which they are set up. It will also encourage you to engage with great force in the practices of giving, morality, patience, and effort, the heart of which is love and compassion. These, in turn, will enhance your capacity for insight. All of these have to work together.

We all have minds that are capable of knowledge; therefore, if you work at it, eventually knowledge can be gained. For this you need to read, listen to lectures, and study; you need long-term thinking; and you need to meditate. Since you are endowed with consciousness and since emptiness is an object that can be brought to mind, your effort will yield results.

Part III

HARNESSING THE POWER OF CONCENTRATION AND INSIGHT

8

Focusing Your Mind

———————

Let distractions melt away like clouds
disappearing in the sky.
—MILAREPA

In all areas of thought, you need to be able to analyze,
and then, when you have come to a decision, you need to
be able to set your mind to it without wavering. These two
capacities—to analyze and to remain focused—are essential to seeing yourself as you really are. In all areas of spiritual development, no matter what your level is, you need
both analysis and focus to achieve the states you are seeking, ranging from seeking a better future, to developing
conviction in the cause and effect of actions (karma), to
developing an intention to leave the round of suffering
called cyclic existence, to cultivating love and compassion,
to realizing the true nature of people and things. All these
improvements are made in the mind by changing how you

think, transforming your outlook through analysis and focus. All types of meditation fall into the general categories of analytical meditation and focusing meditation, also called insight meditation and calm abiding meditation.

If your mind is scattered, it is quite powerless. Distraction here and there opens the way for counterproductive emotions, leading to many kinds of trouble. Without clear, stable concentration, insight cannot know the true nature of phenomena in all its power. For example, to see a painting in the dark, you need a very bright lamp. Even when you have such a lamp, if it is flickering you cannot see the painting clearly and in detail. Also, if the lamp is steady but weak, you cannot see well either. You need both great clarity of mind and steadiness, both insight and focused concentration, like an oil lamp untouched by any breeze. As Buddha said, "When your mind is set in meditative equipoise, you can see reality exactly as it is."

We have nothing but our present mind to accomplish this with, so we must pull the capacities of this mind together to strengthen it. A merchant engages in selling little by little in order to accumulate a pile of money; the capacities of the mind to comprehend facts need to be drawn together and focused in the same way so that the truth can be realized in all its clarity. However, in our usual state we are distracted, like water running everywhere, scattering the innate force of mind in multiple directions, making us incapable of clear perception of the truth. When the mind is not focused, as soon as something appears, it steals away our mind; we run first after this thought and then after that thought, fluctuating and unsteady, powerless to focus on what we want before being pulled away to something else, ready to ruin ourselves. As the Indian scholar-yogi Shantideva says:

> A person whose mind is distracted
> Dwells between the fangs of afflictive emotions.

FOCUSING

Despite the fact that distraction is our current state, the capacities for knowledge which we all possess can be drawn together and focused on an object we want to understand, as we do when we listen to important instructions. Through such focus, all practices—whether love, compassion, the altruistic intention to become enlightened, or insight into your own nature and the actual condition of all other phenomena—are dramatically enhanced, so your progress is much faster and more profound.

Buddhism offers many techniques for developing a form of concentration called "calm abiding." This powerful state of concentration earns its name because in it all distractions have been *calmed* and your mind is—of its own accord—*abiding* continuously, joyously, and flexibly on its chosen internal object with intense clarity and firm stability. At this level of mental development, concentration does not require any exertion at all.

OVERCOMING LAZINESS

Laziness comes in many forms, all of which result in procrastination, putting off practice to another time. Sometimes laziness is a matter of being distracted from meditation by morally neutral activities, like sewing or considering how to drive from one place to another; this type of laziness can be especially pernicious because these thoughts and activities are not usually recognized as problems.

At other times, laziness manifests as distraction to thinking about nonvirtuous activities, such as an object of lust or how to pay an enemy back. Another type of laziness is the sense that you are inadequate to the task of meditation, feeling inferior and discouraged: "How could someone like me ever achieve this!" In this case you are failing to recognize the great potential of the human mind and the power of gradual training.

All of these forms of laziness involve being unenthusiastic about meditation. How can they be overcome? Contemplation of the advantages of attaining mental and physical flexibility will generate enthusiasm for meditation and counteract laziness. Once you have developed the meditative joy and bliss of mental and physical flexibility, you will be able to stay in meditation for as long as you want. At that time your mind will be completely trained so you can direct it to any virtuous activity; all dysfunctions of body and mind will have been cleared away.

CONDITIONS FOR PRACTICE

For beginners, external factors can have considerable impact on meditation because your internal mental capacity is not particularly strong. This is why limiting busy activities and having a quiet place to meditate are helpful. When your internal experience has advanced, external conditions will not affect you much.

At this early stage of cultivating calm abiding, you need a healthful place to practice, away from busy activities and persons who promote lust or anger. Internally, you need to know satisfaction, not having strong desires for food, clothing, and so forth but being satisfied with moderation. You need to limit your activities, giving up commotion. Busyness should be left behind. Of particular importance is moral behavior, which will bring you relaxation, peace, and conscientiousness. All of these preliminaries will help to reduce coarse distractions.

When I became a monk, my vows required limiting my external activities, which placed more emphasis on spiritual development. Restraint made me mindful of my behavior and drew me into considering what was happening in my mind in order to make sure I was not straying from my vows. This meant that even when I was not purposely making an effort at meditation, I kept my mind from being scattered and thus was constantly drawn in the direction of one-pointed, internal meditation.

People sometimes look on vows of morality as confinement or punishment, but that is entirely wrong. Just as we take up a diet to improve our health and not to punish ourselves, so the rules that Buddha laid down are aimed at controlling counterproductive behavior and overcoming afflictive emotions because these are ruinous. For our own sakes, we restrain motivations and deeds that would produce suffering. For example, due to a serious stomach infection I had a few years ago, nowadays I avoid sour foods and cold drinks that otherwise I would enjoy. Such a regimen provides me protection, not punishment.

Buddha set forth styles of behavior in order to improve our welfare, not to give us a hard time. The rules themselves make the mind conducive to spiritual progress.

POSTURE

Meditative posture is important, because if you straighten your body, the energy channels within the body will also straighten, allowing the energy flowing in those channels to balance, which in turn will assist in balancing your mind and putting it at your service. Although meditation could even be conducted lying down, a cross-legged sitting posture with the following seven features is helpful:

1. Sit with your legs crossed, with a separate cushion under your rear.
2. Calm abiding is cultivated by focusing the mind not on an external object but on an internal object. Thus,

with your eyes neither widely open nor tightly closed but open a little, gaze down toward the tip of your nose but not intensely; if this is not comfortable, gaze toward the floor in front of you. Leave your eyes slightly open. Visual stimuli will not bother your mental consciousness. Later, it is fine if your eyes close of their own accord.

3. Straighten your backbone, like an arrow or a pile of coins, without arching back or bending forward.

4. Keep your shoulders level and your hands four finger-widths below the navel, with the left hand underneath, palm up, and the right hand on top of it, also palm up, your thumbs touching to form a triangle.

5. Keep your head level and straight, so that your nose is in a straight line with your navel, but arch your neck slightly, like a peacock.

6. Leave the tip of your tongue touching the roof of your mouth near the front teeth, which later will enable you to stay for long periods in meditation without drooling. It will also keep you from breathing too strongly, which would dry out your mouth and throat.

7. Breathe in and out quietly, gently, and evenly.

A SPECIAL BREATHING PRACTICE

At the start of a session, it is helpful to remove counter-productive currents of energy, called "airs" or "winds," from your body. Like getting rid of rubbish, this series of nine inhalations and exhalations helps to clear away impulses toward lust or hatred that you might have had before the session.

First, inhale deeply through the right nostril by pressing the left nostril closed with your left thumb; then release the left nostril and press your right nostril closed with your left middle finger, exhaling through the left nostril. Do this three times. After that, inhale deeply through the left nostril by continuing to press the right nostril closed with your left middle finger; then release the right nostril and press your left nostril closed with your left thumb, exhaling through the right nostril. Do this three times. Finally, put your left hand back in your lap as described in the previous section and inhale deeply through both nostrils, then exhale through both nostrils. Do this three times, for a total of nine breaths. When inhaling and exhaling, concentrate all of your thought on the inhalations and exhalations, thinking, "inhaling breath" and "exhaling breath," or count each pair of inhalations and exhalations from one to ten and then back to one. Stay focused on your breath, and this in itself will make your mind lighter and vaster, temporarily free from any objects of lust or hatred you might have had, leaving your mind fresh.

At this point, bring your altruistic motivation, your desire to help others, vividly to mind; if you had tried to insert a virtuous attitude earlier, when under the influence of lust or hatred, it would have been difficult, but now it is easier. This breathing practice is like preparing a dirty piece of cloth for dye; after washing, it will easily take the dye.

Concentrating your whole mind just on your breath, which you always have with you and does not need to be newly imagined, will cause earlier thoughts to melt away, making it easier to collect your mind in the subsequent steps.

THE OBJECT

Now let us consider what kind of object you should focus on while practicing to attain calm abiding. Since the effects of previous destructive emotions tend to linger in the back of the mind, any attempt to concentrate your mind is easily interrupted by these forces. If you have already strongly ascertained the emptiness of inherent existence, you could take the image of emptiness as your object of concentration, but initially it is difficult to concentrate on such a deep topic. More typically, you need an object of attention that will weaken your own predominant destructive emotion, whether this is lust, hatred, confusion, pride, or excessive thoughts. The focal points used to counter these tendencies are called "objects for purifying behavior."

If your predominant destructive emotion is lust, you react to even a slightly attractive person or thing with immediate desire. In this case, you can meditate on the components of your body from the top of your head to the soles of your feet—skin, flesh, blood, bone, marrow, urine, feces, and so forth. Seen superficially, the body might be considered beautiful, but if you closely consider its parts for the purposes of this exercise, it is not so beautiful. An eyeball alone can be frightful. Consider everything from your hairs to your fingernails and toenails.

Once when I was visiting Thailand, near the door of a monastery there were pictures of a corpse taken day by day over many days. The stages of decay were obvious; the pictures were really helpful. Your body might seem to be beautiful, with a good tone, solid but soft to the touch; however, when you look closely at its components and the disintegration to which it is susceptible, you see that its nature is different.

If your predominant destructive emotion due to past behavior over many lives is hatred and frustration, meaning you get worked up quickly, and even fly off the handle at others, you can cultivate love through the wish that those who are bereft of happiness be endowed with happiness and the causes of happiness.

If your predominant destructive emotion is confusion and dullness, due, perhaps, to the belief that phenomena occur without causes and conditions, or that the self operates under its own power, you can meditate on the dependent-arising of phenomena, their dependence on causes. You can also contemplate the process of rebirth in cyclic existence, beginning with ignorance and ending with aging and death. Either of these will undermine the confusion of wrong ideas and ignorance and promote intelligence.

If your predominant destructive emotion, carried over from the past, is pride, you can meditate on the categories of phenomena within your mind-body complex. Paying attention to these many factors undermines the sense of a self separate from them. Also, when you consider these in detail, you will realize that there are many things you do not know, thereby deflating your aggrandized sense of self. Nowadays scientists, such as physicists, have their own categories of phenomena, such as the six types of quarks—up, down, charm, strange, top, and bottom—and the four forces—electromagnetic, gravitational, strong nuclear, and weak nuclear—which, if you think you know everything, will puncture your pride when you consider them. You will end up thinking, "I don't know anything."

If your predominant afflictive emotion is generation of too many thoughts, so that you are fluttering around thinking about this and that, you can meditate on the exhalation and inhalation of the breath as described in the previous section. When you tie your mind to the breath, the seemingly ceaseless stream of thoughts roaming here and there will immediately diminish.

If you have no predominant destructive emotion, you can choose any of these objects.

A Special Object

A helpful object of meditation for all personality types is an image of Buddha, or some other religious figure, since concentration on it imbues your mind with virtuous qualities. If by bringing this image to mind again and again you visualize it clearly, it remains with you during all your daily activities, as if you were in a Buddha's presence. When you become sick and are in pain, you will be able to evoke this marvelous presence. Even when you are dying, a Buddha will continuously appear to your mind, and your consciousness of this lifetime will end within an attitude of vivid piety. This would be beneficial, would it not?

In your meditation, imagine an actual Buddha, not a painting or solid statue. First you need to come to know the form of the particular Buddha well through hearing it described or looking at a picture or statue, getting used to it so that an image of it can appear to your mind. For a beginner, mental consciousness is easily scattered here and there to all sorts of objects, but you know from your own experience that if you gaze at an object such as a flower, this scattering will diminish. In the same way, when you gaze at a Buddha-image with your eyes, scattering will lessen, and then gradually you can cause the image to appear to your mind.

Imagine the religious object on the same level as your eyebrows, about five or six feet in front of you; it is one to four inches high. The smaller the object the more it will focus the mind; it should be clear and bright, emitting light but dense. Its brilliance will help to keep the mind's mode of perception from being too loose; its density will help keep the mind from scattering to other objects.

Now the object is fixed with respect to its nature and size for the duration of cultivating calm abiding. You should not switch from these, even though, over time, the image may change in size, color, shape, position, or even number. Put your mind back on the original object.

If you strive too hard to make the object bright and clear, this will interfere; constantly adjusting its brightness will prevent stability from developing. Moderation is needed. Once the object appears even vaguely, stick with it. Later, when the object is steady, you can gradually adjust its brightness and clarity without losing the original image.

Meditative Reflection

1. Look carefully at an image of Buddha, or some other religious figure or symbol, noticing its form, color, and details.
2. Work at causing this image to appear internally to your consciousness, imagining it on the same level as your

eyebrows, about five or six feet in front of you, about one to four inches high (smaller is better), and shining brightly.

3. Consider the image to be real, endowed with magnificent qualities of body, speech, and mind.

9

Tuning Your Mind
for Meditation

A monk named Shrona was trying to meditate, but his
mind was either too tight or too loose. He asked Buddha
for advice. Buddha inquired, "When you were a
householder, did you play the guitar beautifully?"
"Yes, indeed."
"Was the sound right when you tightened the strings hard,
or when you loosened them a lot?"
"Neither. I had to do it with moderation."
"It is the same here. To meditate you have to moderate
the tightness and looseness of your mind."

—PALTRUL RINPOCHE'S *SACRED WORD*

You are seeking to develop a meditative mind that itself
is intensely clear, where consciousness is bright and alert.
You are also seeking the stability of being able to focus
single-mindedly on the object. These are the two qualities
of mind you need: *intense clarity* and *unwavering stability*.

What prevents these from arising? Laxity—the mind's being too loose—prevents the development of clarity, and excitement—the mind's being too tight—prevents staying focused on the object.

LAXITY

There are coarse, subtle, and very subtle forms of laxity. In coarse laxity, the object is not at all clear, and the mind feels sunken, or weighted down. In subtle laxity, you remain on the object, but the mind lacks intense clarity. In very subtle laxity, the intensity is just slightly lacking, the mind being just slightly loose.

Laxity occurs when the mind is withdrawn inside in the process of developing meditation. This is not lethargy, which is a heaviness and unserviceability of mind and body from dullness and which can occur even when attending to an external object. In lethargy your body is heavy, and your mind is heavy, trapped in darkness. Sounds restful, right? Just joking.

EXCITEMENT

Excitement is an agitated state of mind, most often due to an attraction to an external object of lust. It can also be any scattering of the mind, whether the new object is virtuous, such as charity; nonvirtuous, such as lust; or neutral, such as sewing. There are coarse and subtle forms of excitement. In coarse excitement, you forget the object of your meditation and stray off into other thoughts. Although in subtle excitement the object is not lost, a corner of your mind is involved in fast-moving thought, like water flowing under the frozen surface of a river.

In between sessions of meditation, it is important to restrain your senses, to eat a moderate amount of food, and to maintain conscientious introspection of body and mind. Otherwise, these can serve as causes of laxity and excitement. Sleeping too much generally leads to laxity, whereas having unrealistic expectations about the pleasures of life tends to lead to excitement.

LENGTH OF THE SESSION

If you are facing interference to concentration from laxity or excitement and cannot counteract it, rather than stubbornly persisting in long meditation sessions, try short but frequent sessions. When your performance improves and these problems diminish, make the sessions longer.

It helps to meditate in a high place if laxity is a problem, and to meditate at dawn. Just after you wake up, your senses have not yet become active, but the power of thought is present. And because the sense organs are not yet working, you will have fewer distractions. In my own experience, dawn is when my mind is clearest and sharpest.

MINDFULNESS AND INTROSPECTION

Mindfulness is a technique for keeping your mind continuously on the object of your meditation. It is the antidote to forgetfulness. Since beginners have this ability only to a minor degree, you need to train and enhance it by repeatedly putting the mind back on the object.

Frequently check to see whether your mind is on the object or not. By doing this over and over, you will come to notice immediately when your mind has become distracted by something else. Eventually you will notice when your mind is *about* to stray from the object, and you will be able to keep it there. This ability is mindfulness.

The technique for recognizing whether laxity or excitement is preventing the mind from developing clarity and stability is called "introspection." This frequent inspection of whether the object is clear and stable is done not with the full force of the mind but as if from the side, so as not to interfere with the mind's focus on the object.

Indeed, to achieve powerful mindfulness, you need to monitor whether you are staying focused on the object, but the special function of introspection at this point is to see whether the mind has come under the influence of laxity or excitement, not just whether it is staying on the object or not. As the Indian scholar-yogi Bhavaviveka says:

> The elephant of the mind wandering wildly
> Is to be securely bound with the rope of mindfulness
> To the pillar of an object of meditation,
> Gradually to be tamed with the hook of wisdom.

Within your own experience, you need to recognize when your mode of meditation has become too excited or too lax and determine the best practice for adjusting it, as explained in the next two sections. As your faculty of introspection develops, you will gain an inner sense of the right level of tautness, like tuning a guitar string until the right balance is found, neither too sharp nor too flat. Eventually, as a result of your own accumulated experience, you will be able to detect laxity and excitement just before they arise and implement techniques to prevent their arising, tightening or loosening the mind's mode of apprehending the object.

Meditative Reflection

1. Place your mind on the object of meditation.
2. Using introspection, from time to time check to see whether your mind remains on the object.
3. When you find that it has strayed, recall the object and put your mind back on it as often as needed.

In this way you will develop the faculties of mindfulness and introspection.

APPLYING THE REMEDIES

When through introspection you realize that your mind has come under the influence of laxity or excitement or you have a sense that these are about to arise, you need to apply remedies immediately. It is not sufficient just to notice these problems without counteracting them. Remember that failure to enact remedies is itself a problem; make sure to implement them. Do not make the mistake of assuming either that these problems are not important or that you could not possibly stop them.

Remedies to Laxity

In laxity, which is caused by overwithdrawal inside, the mind becomes too relaxed, lacking intensity, the tautness having weakened. Heaviness of mind and body can lead to becoming lax, which can lead to losing the object of observation, as if you have fallen into darkness; this can even turn into sleep. When laxity begins to occur, it is necessary to uplift the mind by making it more taut.

If you need a further technique to intensify the mind, brighten or elevate the object of meditation or pay closer attention to its detail; notice the arch of the eyebrows on the Buddha image if that is your object. If this does not work, then while remaining in meditation, leave the intended object temporarily and think about a topic that makes you joyful, such as the marvelous qualities of love and compassion, or the wonderful opportunity that a human lifetime affords for spiritual practice. If that does not work, and you are still subject to coarse laxity or lethargy, you can even leave off meditating and go to an elevated place, or a place where there is a vast view. Such techniques will cause your deflated mind to heighten and sharpen.

Remedies to Excitement

In times when your mind is excited and you have tried to loosen the tightness of the mind, but this has not worked, you need a further technique to withdraw the mind. At this point, it can help to lower the object and imagine it as heavier. If this does not work, then while continuing to meditate, leave the intended object temporarily and think about a topic that makes you more sober, such as how ignorance induces the sufferings of cyclic existence by putting us under the influence of destructive emotions. Or you could reflect on the imminence of death. It also helps to think about the disadvantages of the object to which you have strayed, and the disadvantages of distraction itself. Such reflections will cause the mind's excessive tightness to loosen a little, making you better able to keep your mind on the object of observation. When that happens, immediately return to the original object. Sometimes I find that if my time for meditation is limited because of work I have to do, this sense of urgency will promote greater exertion in a way that strengthens mindfulness.

DESISTING FROM THE REMEDIES

When you have applied a remedy successfully, it is important to desist from applying it and return your full attention to the object of meditation. Overapplication of antidotes to laxity and excitement when these defects have been removed will itself disrupt the stabilization that you are seeking to achieve. At this point it is crucial to stop applying the remedies and just stay on the object, checking from time to time to see if either excitement or laxity is about to arise.

Later, when you have become highly skilled in meditation and there is no longer any danger of becoming too loose or too tight, even maintaining concern about the possible need to apply remedies will interfere with developing one-pointed concentration. But do not stop being alert to these problems too soon. I will describe in the next section when this is appropriate.

LEVELS OF PROGRESS TOWARD CALM ABIDING

Buddhist teachings describe nine levels of progress toward actual calm abiding; they are a meditation map, telling you where you are and what you need to do to advance.

LEVEL 1: PUTTING THE MIND ON THE OBJECT.

When after hearing or reading instructions on how to set the mind on an object of meditation, you initially draw the mind inside and try to put it there, it may be that you will not be able to keep your mind on the object and will be subject to a waterfall of thoughts, one after another. If so, you are on the first level. You may even have so many thoughts that it seems as if trying to meditate makes them increase, but you are just noticing the previously unidentified extent of your own ramblings. Your attempts at mindfulness are causing you to notice what is happening.

LEVEL 2: PERIODIC PLACEMENT.

As you energetically employ mindfulness and ask yourself again and again, "Am I staying on the object?" you become able to put your mind on the object for brief periods, though there is still more distraction than there is attention to the object. This is the second level, during which rambling thought sometimes takes a rest and sometimes suddenly arises. The main problems during the first two levels come from laziness and forgetting the object, but laxity and excitement also prevent a steady continuum of meditative attention. During the first two levels you are working at *getting* your mind on the object; later you will be working on *keeping* it there.

LEVEL 3: WITHDRAWAL AND RESETTING.

As you gradually come to recognize distraction sooner and sooner through more mindfulness, you become able to place your attention back on the object when it has wandered, as if putting a patch on a cloth. Mindfulness has now matured to the point where you immediately recognize distraction.

LEVEL 4: STAYING CLOSE.

When, due to the full maturation of mindfulness, you are able immediately to counter laziness and forgetfulness, you pass to the fourth level, in which you do not lose the object in forgetfulness. Coarse excitement is over, but subtle versions persist, interfering from time to time though not causing you to lose the object. On the first three levels, laziness and forgetfulness were the main problems, but now laxity and excitement have become the chief concerns.

LEVEL 5: DISCIPLINING THE MIND.

Introspection now becomes stronger, and through your own experience you recognize the advantages of meditative stability; coarse laxity no longer arises. The withdrawal of the mind from extraneous objects now proceeds too far, so it becomes necessary to apply remedies to subtle laxity and thereby heighten the mind.

LEVEL 6: PACIFYING THE MIND.

By applying remedies to subtle laxity, you attain the sixth level. Introspection has fully developed, and through your own experience you know the faults of scattering to thoughts and destructive emotions; subtle laxity poses no great danger. However, those very remedies for overcoming subtle laxity by heightening the mind may lead to an overly invigorated mind, and now there is danger of generating subtle excitement.

LEVEL 7: THOROUGHLY PACIFYING THE MIND.

By applying remedies to subtle excitement, you reach the seventh level. As soon as desire, scattering, laxity, lethargy, and the like are produced in even subtle form, you abandon them through exertion. Now you no longer need to be concerned about coming under the influence of subtle laxity and excitement. Effort is now able to stop laxity and excitement so that they cannot damage your concentration, even if they make slight interruptions.

LEVEL 8: MAKING THE MIND ONE-POINTED.

Now the power of effort has fully matured so that, with a little exertion at the beginning of the session, the entire session of meditation remains devoid of laxity and excitement, and you are able to maintain meditative stability without interruption. Analyzing whether laxity or excitement are about to arise is no longer needed during the session. Now such exertion can be set aside, but this does not mean loosening the intensely clear mode of perceiving the object.

LEVEL 9: THE MIND PLACED IN EQUIPOISE.

Now that you have gained the power of familiarity from this training, the exertion of implementing mindfulness and introspection is no longer needed, and the mind places itself on the object of its own accord; the ninth level is spontaneous. When at the start of a session you set your mind on the object, meditative stability is sustained without interruption for a long time through its own force, without needing to rely even on the slight initial exertion required on the previous level. You now have no need to apply remedies to any type of laxity or excitement.

FEATURES OF CALM ABIDING

The ninth level, despite being spontaneous, still precedes the level of calm abiding. Through further cultivation of one-pointed attention free from the defects of laxity and excitement, flexibility of mind and body is generated.

First, your brain feels heavy, though not in an unpleasant way. Also, a tingly sensation is felt at the top of the head, like the feeling of a warm hand put on top of the head after it has been shaved. This is a sign that the *mental flexibility* that removes mental dysfunctions preventing completely easy meditative focus is about to be generated. It is a mental lightness generated only from meditation when the mind happily stays on its object.

This mental flexibility causes a favorable energy to circulate throughout the body, producing a *physical flexibility* removing all physical awkwardness and dysfunction that leads to fatigue and a lack of enthusiasm for meditation. Your body feels light, like cotton. This physical flexibility immediately engenders a *bliss of physical flexibility*, a feeling of comfort pervading the body. Now you can use your body in virtuous activities in accordance with your wish.

This physical pleasure leads to mental pleasure, called "bliss of mental flexibility," making the mind full of joy that initially is a little too buoyant but gradually becomes more steady. At this juncture you attain an *unfluctuating flexibility*. This marks the achievement of true calm abiding. Before this, you have only a similitude of calm abiding.

With fully qualified calm abiding, your mind is powerfully concentrated enough to purify destructive emotions when it is joined with insight. When you enter into meditative equipoise, mental and physical flexibility are quickly generated, and it is as if your mind is mixed with space itself. When you leave meditation, your body is like new to you, and aspects of mental and physical flexibility remain. Outside meditation, your mind is firm like a mountain and so clear that it seems you could count the particles in a wall, and you have fewer counterproductive emotions, being mostly free from desire for pleasant sights, sounds, odors, tastes, and touches, as well as free from harmful intent, lethargy, sleepiness, excitement, contrition, and doubt. Also, sleep easily turns into meditation, in which you have many wonderful experiences.

Meditative Reflection

1. To counter laxity, which is a too-loose way of perceiving the meditative object:

> First try to tighten just a little your way of holding the object.
>
> If that does not work, brighten or elevate the object or pay closer attention to its details.
>
> If that does not work, leave the intended object and temporarily think about a joyous topic, such as the marvelous qualities of love and compassion or the wonderful opportunity that a human lifetime affords for spiritual practice.
>
> If that does not work, leave off meditating and go to a high place or one where there is a vast view.

2. To counter excitement, which is a too-tight way of
perceiving the meditative object:

> First try to loosen just a little your way of imagining
> the object.
>
> If that does not work, lower the object in your mind
> and imagine it as heavier.
>
> If that does not work, leave the intended object and
> temporarily think about a topic that makes you
> more sober, such as how ignorance brings about
> the sufferings of cyclic existence, or the immi-
> nence of death, or the disadvantages of the object
> to which you have strayed and the disadvantages
> of distraction itself.

By learning these techniques you will gradually develop
the ability to apply them when you notice problems with
your quality of attention while meditating.

Part IV

HOW TO END
SELF-DECEPTION

Meditating on Yourself

Since it is the individual person who undergoes pleasure
and pain, makes trouble, and is capable of learning, all
the advice and the most loving meditations one can learn
should begin with yourself. Then, when we realize ... and
that the person really ... others ... ...
... ...
and feelings of for this inner ...
This is why ... the ... of ...
of persons and those who are ... ...
ness of phenomena. His *Precious Garland*, Nāgārjuna

A person is not earth, not water,
Nor fire, nor wind, nor space.

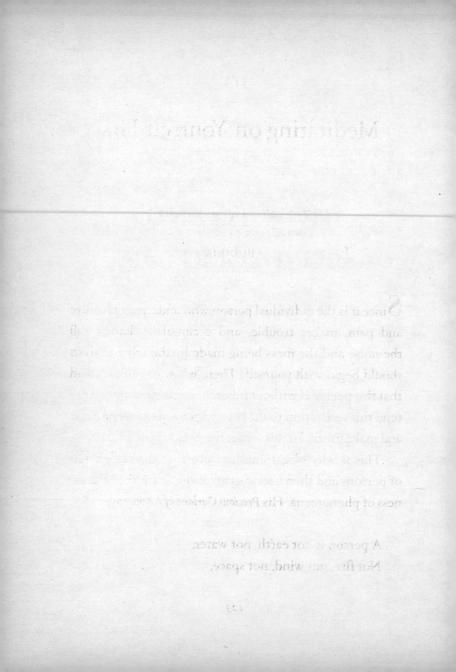

10

Meditating on Yourself First

Through one all are known.
Through one all are also seen.

—BUDDHA

Since it is the individual person who undergoes pleasure and pain, makes trouble, and accumulates karma—all the noise and the mess being made by the self—analysis should begin with yourself. Then, when you understand that this person is without inherent existence, you can extend this realization to the things that you enjoy, undergo, and make use of. In this sense, the person is principal.

This is why Nagarjuna first presents the selflessness of persons and then uses it as an example for the selflessness of phenomena. His *Precious Garland of Advice* says:

A person is not earth, not water,
Not fire, not wind, not space,

Not consciousness, and not all of them.
What person is there other than these?

Just as due to being set up in dependence upon an
    aggregation of the six constituents
A person is not established as its own reality,
So due to being set up in dependence upon an
    aggregation
Each of the constituents also is not established as its
    own reality.

Just as a person does not inherently exist because he or she
is dependent upon a collection of the six constituents—
earth (the hard substances of the body), water (fluids),
fire (heat), wind (energy, movement), space (the hollow
places in the body), and consciousness—so it is that each
of the constituents also does not inherently exist because
it, in turn, is set up in dependence upon its own parts.

Examples are easier to understand than what they ex-
emplify. Buddha speaks to this in the *King of Meditations
Sutra*:

Just as you have come to know the false
    discrimination of yourself,

Apply this mentally to all phenomena.
All phenomena are completely devoid
Of their own inherent existence, like space.
Through one all are known.
Through one all are also seen.

When you know well how the "I" really is, you can understand all internal and external phenomena using the same reasoning. Seeing how one phenomenon—yourself—exists, you can also know the nature of all other phenomena. This is why the procedure for meditation is first to strive to generate realization of your own lack of inherent existence and then to work at realizing the same with respect to other phenomena.

Meditative Reflection

Consider:

1. The person is at the center of all troubles.
2. Therefore, it is best to work at understanding your true nature first.
3. After that, this realization can be applied to mind, body, house, car, money, and all other phenomena.

II

Realizing That You Do Not Exist in and of Yourself

Just as a chariot is verbalized
In dependence on collections of parts,
So conventionally a sentient being
Is set up depending on the mental and physical aggregates.

—BUDDHA

In Buddhism the term *self* has two meanings that must be differentiated in order to avoid confusion. One meaning of *self* is "person," or "living being." This is the being who loves and hates, who performs actions and accumulates good and bad karma, who experiences the fruits of those actions, who is reborn in cyclic existence, who cultivates spiritual paths, and so on.

The other meaning of *self* occurs in the term *selflessness,* where it refers to a falsely imagined, overconcretized status of existence called "inherent existence." The ignorance that adheres to such an exaggeration is indeed the source of ruination, the mother of all wrong attitudes—perhaps we could even say devilish. In observing the "I" that depends upon mental and physical attributes, this mind exaggerates it into being inherently existent, despite the fact that the mental and physical elements being observed do not contain any such exaggerated being.

What is the actual status of a sentient being? Just as a car exists in dependence upon its parts, such as wheels, axles, and so forth, so a sentient being is conventionally set up in dependence upon mind and body. There is no person to be found either separate from mind and body or within mind and body.

NAME-ONLY

This is the reason why the "I" and all other phenomena are described in Buddhism as "name-only." The meaning of this is not that the "I" and all other phenomena are just words, since the words for these phenomena do indeed refer to actual objects. Rather, these phenomena do not exist in and of themselves; the term *name-only* eliminates the possibility that they are established from the object's own side. We need this reminder because the "I" and other phenomena do not appear to be merely set up by name and thought. Quite the contrary.

For instance, we say that the Dalai Lama is a monk, a human, and a Tibetan. Does it not seem that you are saying this not with respect to his body or his mind but about something separate? Without stopping to think about it, it seems that there is a Dalai Lama that is separate from his body, and independent even of his mind. Or consider yourself. If your name is Jane, for instance, we say, "Jane's body, Jane's mind," so it seems to you that there is a Jane who owns her mind and body, and a mind and body that Jane owns.

How can you understand that this perspective is mistaken? Focus on the fact that there is nothing within mind and body that can be "I." Mind and body are empty of a tangible "I." Rather, just as a car is set up *in dependence upon* its parts and is not even the sum of its parts, so the "I" depends upon mind and body. An "I" without depending on mind and body does not exist, whereas an "I" that is understood to be dependent upon mind and body exists in accordance with the conventions of the world. Understanding this type of "I" that is not at all to be found within mind and body, and is not even the sum of mind and body but exists only through the power of its name and our thoughts, is helpful as we strive to see ourselves as we really are.

FOUR STEPS TO REALIZATION

There are four major steps toward realizing that you do not exist the way you think you do. I will discuss these briefly first, and then in detail.

The first step is to identify the ignorant beliefs that must be refuted. You need to do this because when you perform analysis seeking yourself within mind and body or separate from mind and body, and you do not find it, you could wrongly conclude that you utterly do not exist.

Because the "I" appears to our minds to be established in and of itself, when we use analysis to try to find it and it is not found, it seems that the "I" does not exist at all, whereas it is only the independent "I," the inherently existent "I," that does not exist. Because there is a danger here of stumbling into denial and nihilism, it is crucial as a first step to understand what is being negated in selflessness.

How does "I" appear to your mind? It does not appear

to exist through the force of thought; rather, it appears to exist more concretely. You need to notice and identify this mode of apprehension. It is your target.

The second step is to determine that, if the "I" exists the way it seems to be, it must be either one with mind and body or separate from mind and body. After ascertaining that there are no other possibilities, in *the final two steps* you analyze to see whether the "I" and the mind-body complex can be either one inherently established entity or different inherently established entities.

As we will discuss in the following sections, through meditation you gradually will come to understand that there are fallacies with "I" being either of these. At that point you can readily realize that an inherently existent "I" is unfounded. This is realization of selflessness. Then, when you have realized that the "I" does not inherently exist, it is easy to realize that what is "mine" does not inherently exist.

THE FIRST STEP:
IDENTIFYING THE TARGET

Usually, no matter what appears to our minds, it seems to exist from its own side, independent of thought. When we pay attention to an object—whether it be yourself, another person, body, mind, or a material thing—we accept how it appears as if this is its final, inner, real condition. This can be clearly seen at times of stress, such as when someone else criticizes you for something you have not done: "You ruined such-and-such." You suddenly think very strongly "*I* didn't do that!" And you might even shout this at the accuser.

How does "I" appear to your mind at that moment? How does this "I" that you value and cherish so much seem to exist? How are you apprehending it? By reflecting on these questions you can get a sense of the way the mind naturally and innately apprehends "I" as existing from its own side, inherently.

Let us take another example. When there is something important you were supposed to do and you discover that you forgot to do it, you can get angry at your own mind: "Oh, my awful memory!" When you get angry at your own mind, the "I" that is angry and the mind at which you are angry appear to be separate from each other.

The same thing happens when you get upset with your body, or a part of your body, such as your hand. The "I" that is angry seems to have its own being, in and of itself, distinct from the body at which you are angry. On such occasions you can observe how the "I" seems to stand by itself, as if it is self-instituting, as if it is established by way of its own character. To such a consciousness, the "I" does not appear to be set up in dependence upon mind and body.

Can you remember a time when you did something awful and your mind thought, "I really made a mess of things"? At that moment you identified with a sense of "I" that has its own concrete entity, that is neither mind nor body but something that appears much more strongly.

Or remember a time when you did something wonderful or something really nice happened to you, and you took great pride in it. This "I" that is so valued, so cherished, so liked, and is the object of such self-importance was so concretely and vividly clear. At such times, our sense of "I" is particularly obvious.

Once you catch hold of such a blatant manifestation, you can cause this strong sense of "I" to appear to your mind, and without letting the way it seems diminish in strength, you can examine, as if from a corner, whether it exists in the solid way it appears. In the seventeenth century, the Fifth Dalai Lama spoke about this with great clarity:

Sometimes the "I" will seem to exist in the context of the body. Sometimes it will seem to exist in the context of the mind. Sometimes it will seem to exist in the context of feelings, discriminations, or other factors. At the end of noticing a variety of modes of appearance, you will come to identify an "I" that exists in its own right, that exists inherently, that from the start is self-established, existing undifferentiatedly with mind and body, which are also mixed like milk and water. This is the first step, ascertainment of the object to be negated in the view of selflessness. You should work at it until deep experience arises.

The remaining three steps, discussed in the following three chapters, are aimed at understanding that this sort of "I," which we believe in so much and which drives so much of our behavior, actually is a figment of the imagination. This solid "I" does not exist at all. For the subsequent steps to work, it is crucial to identify and stay with this strong sense of a self-instituting "I."

Meditative Reflection

1. Imagine that someone else criticizes you for something you actually have not done, pointing a finger at you and saying, "You ruined such-and-such."
2. Watch your reaction. How does the "I" appear to your mind?
3. In what way are you apprehending it?
4. Notice how that "I" seems to stand by itself, self-instituting, established by way of its own character.

Also:

1. Remember a time when you were fed up with your mind, such as when you failed to remember something.
2. Review your feelings. How did the "I" appear to your mind at that time?
3. In what way were you apprehending it?
4. Notice how that "I" seems to stand by itself, self-instituting, established by way of its own character.

Also:

1. Remember a time when you were fed up with your body, or with some feature of your body, such as your hair.

2. Look at your feelings. How did the "I" appear to your mind at that time?
3. In what way were you apprchending it?
4. Notice how that "I" seems to stand by itself, self-instituting, established by way of its own character.

Also:

1. Remember a time when you did something awful and you thought, "I really made a mess of things."
2. Consider your feelings. How did the "I" appear to your mind at that time?
3. In what way were you apprehending it?
4. Notice how that "I" seems to stand by itself, self-instituting, established by way of its own character.

Also:

1. Remember a time when you did something wonderful and you took great pride in it.
2. Examine your feelings. How did the "I" appear to your mind at that time?
3. In what way were you apprehending it?
4. Notice how that "I" seems to stand by itself, self-instituting, established by way of its own character.

Also:

1. Remember a time when something wonderful happened to you and you took great pleasure in it.
2. Watch your feelings. How did the "I" appear to your mind at that time?
3. In what way were you apprehending it?
4. Notice how that "I" seems to stand by itself, self-instituting, established by way of its own character.

12

Determining the Choices

When phenomena are individually analyzed as selfless
And what has been analyzed is meditated upon,
That is the cause for attaining the fruit, nirvana.
One does not go to peace through any other cause.

—BUDDHA

In the first step, you figured out how you appear to your
mind. This realization was necessary because if you do not
get a sense of what inherent existence is, no matter how
much you might talk about selflessness or emptiness, it
would be just words. After you have identified the sense
that objects exist from power within themselves, then
when you study about and meditate on selflessness and
emptiness, the way is open for some understanding of the
absence of overconcretized existence to dawn to your
mind. However, without knowing how objects appear to
have such a status and how you assent to it, you might have

the impression that the great treatises on emptiness are just trying to force us to accept what they are saying. Therefore, keep coming back to the first step, since as your knowledge deepens, your estimation of the target being investigated will become more and more subtle.

THE SECOND STEP:
LIMITING THE POSSIBILITIES

Now you need to establish a logical structure for the subsequent analysis. In general, anything that you take to mind has to be either one or more than one, singular or plural. For instance, it is obvious that a stone pillar and an iron pot are plural; a bowl is one thing, singular.

Because this is the case, what is inherently established must also be either one entity or different entities; there is no other possibility. This means that if the "I" inherently exists, it must be either one with the mind and body or entirely different from the mind and body.

You need to ponder these parameters. They are the context for examining in the last two steps whether the target that you identified in the first step really does exist so concretely. If it does, it should be able to withstand this analysis.

Meditative Reflection

1. Analyze whether the "I" that is inherently self-established in the context of the mind-body complex could have a way of existing other than being part of or separate from mind and body.

2. Take other phenomena, such as a cup and a table, or a house and a mountain, as examples. See that there is no third category of existence. They are either the same or different.

3. Decide that if the "I" inherently exists as it seems to, it must be either one with or separate from mind and body.

13

Analyzing Oneness

The doctrine supremely purifying the mind
Is the absence of inherent existence.

—NAGARJUNA'S *PRAISE OF REALITY*

Now you are ready to analyze whether the "I" could be one with mind and body. Consider the following implications. If the "I" is established in and of itself, as it appears to our minds, and if it also is the same as mind-body, then "I" and mind-body could not differ at all. They would have to be utterly and in all ways the same. Phenomena that appear one way but exist another way are false, but it is impossible for what is truly established to have a conflict between appearance and actual fact. What is true must appear the way it exists and must exist the way it appears.

If the "I" is the same as mind-body, does it even make sense to assert the existence of the "I"? As Nagarjuna's *Treatise on the Middle* says:

When it is taken that there is no self
Except the mind-body complex,
Then the mind-body complex itself would be
    the self.
If so, your self is nonexistent.

If "I" and the mind-body complex are exactly the same, it would be impossible to think of "my body" or "my head" or "my mind" or surmise that "my body is getting stronger." Also, if the self and mind-body are one, then when mind and body no longer exist, the self also would not exist.

A second problem is that, since mind and body are plural, one person's selves also would have to be manifold. As Chandrakirti says:

If mind and body were the self,
Then because mind and body are plural
The selves would also just be plural.

Or, just as the self is one, mind and body also would absurdly be one.

A third problem is that, just as mind and body are produced and disintegrate, the "I" would have to be inherently produced and inherently disintegrate. Although Buddhists accept that the self is produced and disintegrates, we hold that this is so *conventionally,* not inherently from its own side. In the absence of inherent existence, it is possible for a series of moments, and even lives, to form a continuum in which later depends on earlier. However, if the self is inherently produced and inherently disintegrates, it would be impossible for the present moments of your life to depend on former moments, since each moment would be produced and disintegrate in and of itself, without depending on anything else. In this case, former lifetimes would be impossible, since each life would exist in and of itself.

Buddha spoke of remembering former lifetimes, and some mistakenly take this to mean that the Buddha after enlightenment and the individual he was in a former lifetime are one and the same, and thus permanent. However, when Buddha described earlier lifetimes, he was careful not to specify that the person of his present life in a particular place at a particular time was the former person in a particular place at a particular time. He spoke in general terms, saying merely, "In the past I was such-and-such a person," but he did not say, "In the past Shakyamuni Buddha was such-and-such a person."

In this way the agent of actions (karma) in a former lifetime and the agent that experiences the results of those karmas are included within the continuum of what Buddhists call the "noninherently existent I" (or "mere-I") that travels from lifetime to lifetime. Otherwise, if the "I" were inherently produced and inherently disintegrates, such continuity would be impossible, since the two lives—the person who committed the action and the person undergoing the effect—would be unrelated. This would result in the absurdity that the pleasurable effects of virtuous actions and the painful effects of nonvirtuous actions would not bear fruition for us; the effects of those actions would be wasted. Also, since we undeniably experience the effects of actions, we would be experiencing the effects of actions we ourselves did not commit.

Meditative Reflection

Consider the consequences if the "I" is established in and of itself in accordance with how it appears to our minds and if it also is the same as mind-body:

1. "I" and mind-body would have to be utterly and in all ways one.
2. In that case, asserting an "I" would be pointless.

3. It would be impossible to think of "my body" or "my head" or "my mind."

4. When mind and body no longer exist, the self also would not exist.

5. Since mind and body are plural, one person's selves also would be plural.

6. Since the "I" is just one, mind and body also would be one.

7. Just as mind and body are produced and disintegrate, so it would have to be asserted that the "I" is inherently produced and inherently disintegrates. In this case, neither the pleasurable effects of virtuous actions nor the painful effects of nonvirtuous actions would bear fruit for us, or we would be experiencing the effects of actions we ourselves did not commit.

Remember, what is inherently established cannot be included within the same continuum but must be unrelatedly different. Understanding this depends on getting an accurate sense of how the "I" and other phenomena usually appear to you to be self-instituting, and how you usually accept that appearance and then act on the basis of it. This is the kind of exaggerated existence we are investigating.

14

Analyzing Difference

Just as it is known
That an image of one's face is seen
Depending on a mirror
But does not really exist as a face,
So the conception of "I" exists
Dependent on mind and body,
But like the image of a face
The "I" does not at all exist as its own reality.

—NAGARJUNA'S *PRECIOUS GARLAND OF ADVICE*

Now analyze whether the "I" and mind-body could be different. Consider the following implications. Mental and physical things are called "compound phenomena" because they are produced, abide, and disintegrate moment by moment. These characteristics reveal that mental and physical factors exist due to specific causes and conditions, and are therefore impermanent.

If the "I" and the whole range of impermanent phenomena were inherently different, the "I" would absurdly not have the characteristics of impermanent phenomena, namely, being produced, abiding, and disintegrating, just as a horse, because of being a different entity from an elephant, does not have the particular features of an elephant. As Chandrakirti says:

> If the self is asserted to be different from mind and body, then just as consciousness is different from body, the self would be established as having a character entirely different from mind and body.

Again, if the "I" and mind-body were inherently different, the "I" would have to be something falsely imagined or a permanent phenomenon. It also could not have the particular characteristics of either body or mind, and thus would have to be observed entirely separately from body and mind. When you search for what the "I" is, you would have to come up with something separate from mind and body, but you cannot. The "I" is perceived only in the context of mind and body. As Chandrakirti says:

> There is no self other than the mind-body complex because

Apart from the mind-body complex, its conception
does not exist.

Meditative Reflection

Consider the consequences if the "I" is established in and
of itself in accordance with how it appears to our minds
and if it also is inherently different from mind-body:

1. "I" and mind-body would have to be completely separate.
2. In that case, the "I" would have to be findable after
   clearing away mind and body.
3. The "I" would not have the characteristics of production, abiding, and disintegration, which is absurd.
4. The "I" would absurdly have to be just a figment of
   the imagination or permanent.
5. Absurdly, the "I" would not have any physical or mental characteristics.

15

Coming to a Conclusion

The reality is later ascertained
Of what was formerly imagined by ignorance.
—NAGARJUNA'S *PRECIOUS GARLAND OF ADVICE*

In the middle of the seventeenth century, the Fifth Dalai Lama emphasized how important it is for analysis not to become rote but to be lively. When you search for such a concretely existent "I" and do not find it as either the same as or inherently different from mind and body, it is crucial that the search be thorough; otherwise, you will not feel the impact of not finding it. The Fifth Dalai Lama wrote:

It is not sufficient that the mode of nonfinding be just a repetition of the impoverished phrase "not found." For example, when an ox is lost, one does not take as true the mere statement, "It is not in such-and-such an area." Rather, by thoroughly searching for it in the highland, midland, and lowland of the area, you come to a firm decision that it cannot be found. Here also, through meditating until a conclusion is reached, you gain conviction.

Once you engage in analyzing in this way, you will begin to question the strong sense of a self-instituting "I" that earlier seemed to exist so palpably. You will gradually start to think, "Aha! Previously this seemed to be so true, but maybe it really isn't." Then, as you analyze more and more, you will become convinced (not just superficially but from the depths) that such an "I" does not exist at all. You will pass beyond mere words and gain conviction that, though it appears so concretely, it does not exist that way. This is the imprint of extended analysis: a decision from within your own mind that this sort of "I" really does not exist.

Often when I am about to give a lecture to a large number of people, I notice that to my mind each person in the audience seems to exist on his or her own respective seat through his or her own power, rather than existing only through the power of thought, existing only conventionally. They all seem to exist in a condition of exaggerated solidity; this is how they seem, how they appear, how they dawn to my mind. But if they did exist this way, they would have to be findable through the type of examination I have just described, whereas they cannot. There is a conflict between how they appear and how they actually exist. Therefore, I call to mind whatever I know about selflessness, reflecting, for instance, on Nagarjuna's statement in his *Fundamental Treatise on the Middle Called "Wisdom,"* where he examines whether the Buddha inherently exists:

> The Buddha is not his mind-body complex.
> He is not other than his mind-body complex.
> The mind-body complex is not in him; he is not in it.
> He does not possess it. What Buddha is there?

Nagarjuna uses the Buddha as an example of being selfless, of the absence of an inherently existent person. In the same way, we need to reflect on our own selflessness. When I apply this reflection to myself, I think:

> The monk Tenzin Gyatso is not his mind-body complex.
> He is not other than his mind-body complex.

The mind-body complex is not in him; he is not in it. He does not possess it. What Tenzin Gyatso is there?

The monk Tenzin Gyatso is not anything in his mind-body complex, ranging from the top of his head to the soles of his feet. When I seek the monk Tenzin Gyatso, nothing is found—not the visual consciousness, not the hearing consciousness, not the smelling consciousness, not the tasting consciousness, not the body consciousness, and not the mental consciousness; not the waking consciousness, not the dreaming consciousness, not the consciousness of deep sleep, and at the end not even the clear light of death. Are any of these Tenzin Gyatso? None is found to be Tenzin Gyatso.

Also, there is nothing outside of the mind-body complex that is Tenzin Gyatso. In addition, Tenzin Gyatso does not depend on the mind-body complex as a separate entity, like a lion in a grove of trees; also, the mind-body complex does not depend on Tenzin Gyatso as a separate entity, like a forest of trees in snow; both of those would require that Tenzin Gyatso and the mind-body complex be different entities, and that is impossible. Also, Tenzin Gyatso does not possess the mind-body complex, like a person possessing a cow, which would require different entities, or like a tree possessing its core, which would be the same entity.

Then what Tenzin Gyatso is there? For sure, nothing can be found—not as part of the mind-body complex, not depending on the mind-body complex as a separate entity, not in possession of the mind-body complex, and not even as the continuum of the mind-body complex. It is clear that the self is merely set up in dependence upon the mind-body complex.

This analysis stands in opposition to the way we usually think. When I think, "I am a monk," there is an appearance in my mind of the monk to whom body and mind belong. We are all humans, that is for sure, but when we identify ourselves as a person and when we identify someone else as a different person over there, these two appear most concretely. Yet when we apply analysis to determine what the actual person is—when we analyze whether this person is a certain type of mind and body—we do not come up with anything that is the person. Also, it is not possible for something entirely separate from mind and body to be the person. This being the case, this profound Buddhist system teaches us that a person is just set up in dependence upon mind and body.

When I use analysis, I understand that what originally seemed to be so palpable does not at all exist this way. The person that appeared to exist so forthrightly just plain cannot be found. This which seemed to exist in itself is seen to depend on thought.

Reflecting on this, when I look out at an audience, I see that all these tens of thousands of people are thinking "I," "I," "I," "I" in a way that in fact is mistaken, drawing themselves into trouble. Seeing them this way helps me— and will help you—call forth loving concern for beings trapped in misconception. This is often how I begin my lectures.

By meditating and gradually cultivating these four steps, you will develop an ability to examine anything and everything this way—seeing the conflict between appearance and reality, and deciding from the depths that persons and things do not exist the way they appear. What is understood by that completely decisive mind is the absence of the inherently existent "I," even though you used to believe in it so strongly. You totally understand the negation of inherent existence. Your mind becomes absorbed in that emptiness.

Meditative Reflection

Repeatedly review the four steps to realization:

1. Zero in on the target, the appearance of the "I" as if it is established in and of itself.

2. Determine that if the "I" exists the way it seems to, it must be either one with mind and body or separate from mind and body.

3. Thoroughly contemplate the problems with "I" and the mind-body complex being the same.

   - "I" and mind-body would have to be utterly and in all ways one.
   - Asserting an "I" would be pointless.
   - It would be impossible to think of "my body" or "my head" or "my mind."
   - When mind and body no longer exist, the self also would not exist.
   - Since mind and body are plural, a person's selves also would be plural.
   - Since the "I" is just one, mind and body also would be one.
   - Just as mind and body are produced and disinte-

grate, the "I" is inherently produced and inherently disintegrates. In this case, neither the pleasurable effects of virtuous actions nor the painful effects of nonvirtuous actions would bear fruit for us, or we would be experiencing the effects of actions we ourselves did not commit.

4. Thoroughly contemplate the problems with "I" and the mind-body complex being inherently different.

- "I" and mind-body would have to be completely separate.
- In that case, the "I" would have to be findable after clearing away mind and body.
- The "I" would not have the characteristics of production, abiding, and disintegration, which is absurd.
- The "I" would absurdly have to be just a figment of the imagination or permanent.
- Absurdly, the "I" would not have any physical or mental characteristics.

16

Testing Your Realization

Just as one comes to ruin
Through wrong eating but obtains
Long life, freedom from disease,
Strength, and pleasures through right eating,
So one comes to ruin
Through wrong understanding
But attains happiness and highest enlightenment
Through right understanding.

—NAGARJUNA'S *PRECIOUS GARLAND OF ADVICE*

When you have done analysis with respect to yourself, searching for an inherently existent "I," eventually you experience a nonfinding of "I," but is this the emptiness of inherent existence or something coarser? We call the coarser level a person's "not being substantially existent in the sense of being self-sufficient" and the subtler level a person's "not being inherently existent." It is possible to mistakenly conclude that you have understood the subtler emptiness when you have actually understood only the coarser one.

Both realizations are helpful, and understanding the coarser will certainly help toward realizing the subtler, but it is important not to confuse the two. To tell the difference, first go through the reasoning summarized in Chapter 15; then when the sense that the "I" is self-instituting falls apart, and it vanishes for your mind in a vacuum, switch the topic of your investigation from the "I" to your body, or some part of the body, such as your arm.

If your sense that your body or arm is self-instituting immediately vanishes, and the absence of such a status appears to your mind, this is a sign that your understanding of the emptiness of the "I" has been on the subtler level. However, if the force of the previous reasoning does not immediately apply to your body or arm, this shows that your understanding of the emptiness of the "I" is not so deep but is on a coarser level.

If some sense of the concrete existence of this other phenomenon remains, your earlier analysis was not as deep as it might have seemed. This is why Nagarjuna says:

> As long as mind and body are misapprehended,
> So long therefore does the misapprehension of "I" exist.

HOW TO TELL THE DIFFERENCE BETWEEN COARSE AND SUBTLE MISCONCEPTIONS

A possible reason for the understanding of "I" not to extend to other phenomena is that the initial identification of a self-instituting "I" was done in the context of a *blatant* instance of exaggeration of yourself, to which you reacted with lust, hatred, defensiveness, or the like. Based on that coarse identification, it might seem that in ordinary circumstances your sense of "I" is not mixed with an appearance of a self-instituting "I." But in fact it is, although on a subtler level. This is why the original realization, although helpful, does not have as much force as it could.

I want to go into some detail on this point, so please bear with me. We first need to consider this intriguing question: If a person is neither body nor mind, or a combination of these two, or something other than these elements, then what are we looking at when we consider "I"? Our texts tell us that what we are paying attention to is a dependently set up "I" or person. We are paying attention to, though not properly understanding, just the "I," which Buddhists call the "mere-I." Because misconstruing mind and body as inherently existent so quickly precedes our misapprehension of "I," it can seem that what we are paying attention to when we consider "I" is mind and body, but actually it is the "I" itself.

Nevertheless, the fact is that, no matter what now appears to our minds, whether to our senses or to our mental consciousness, it is mixed with an exaggeration of its condition. All appearances of external and internal objects, including "I," are mixed with a sense that the objects exist from their own side; for this reason, all of our consciousnesses are mistaken with respect to what appears to them, even when they are right about certain observations, such as seeing a blue object as blue, or identifying a door as a door. Such minds are right about the general objects but mistaken in that, because of our own predispositions, the objects are seen with an overlay of inherent existence.

Therefore, if when meditating you accept the appearance of yourself as it is and proceed to refute some additional sense of inherent existence, you have already overlooked a prime example of the inherent existence that you are seeking to refute. Yes, you do exist, but this "I" does not exist in the way it appears to your mind. This is why the seventeenth-century First Panchen Lama emphasized that inherent existence must be refuted with respect to that very first "I" that usually appears.

This "I" does not exist. When this fact is seen, the root misconception is counteracted, whereas if you leave that "I" as if it exists and continue with your analysis, you will not get down to the level of the root problem. This is because the "mere-I" (the noninherently existent "I") and the inherently existent "I" are presently blended together. Therefore, you have to consider that this "I" that you are paying attention to does not exist as it appears. Otherwise, if you take this "I" to be real and seek only to prove that it does not *ultimately* exist, your will misunderstand the nature of its emptiness, as explained in Chapter 7.

PERSISTENCE IS NEEDED

The need to proceed to this deeper level is why you must keep working at alternating between identifying a more and more subtle sense of how that "I" appears and using reasoning to see if that appearance can bear analysis. Through this process you will gradually deepen your comprehension of both what an exaggerated sense of self is and the shakiness of its foundation.

Just as the great texts say, you will begin to make a distinction between existence and inherent existence through your own experience. The great texts challenge us to avoid both the extreme of exaggerating the nature of persons and things and the opposite extreme—that people and things do not exist at all. They definitely do exist; how they exist is the issue.

When you advance toward understanding that people and things cannot be found under analysis but take to mind that they do indeed exist, you may begin to feel the impact of the statement that they exist through the power of thought. This, in turn, will challenge you to consider further how people and things appear to your mind and will undermine your confidence in the goodness or badness of these appearances, which you previously automatically accepted as intrinsic to the objects. You will begin noticing how you assent to the appearance of objects and how you latch on to them.

In this way, meditation is a long journey, not a single insight or even several insights. It gets more and more profound as the days, months, and years pass. Keep reading and thinking and meditating.

Meditative Reflection

1. Go through the four steps of analysis described in Chapter 15.
2. When the sense that the "I" is self-instituting falls

apart and vanishes in a void, switch to considering your arm, for instance.

3. See whether the sense that your arm inherently exists immediately vanishes due to the previous reasoning.

4. If the previous analysis does not immediately apply to your arm, your understanding is still on a coarser level.

KEEP WORKING AT IT

The sign that you have truly become impressed with the absence of the concrete, solid existence of the "I" occurs when you consider body or mind and no longer take their appearance to be true. You cease investing so much confidence in their exaggerated appearances because you have become impressed with the absence of inherent existence discovered through meditative analysis. This diminishing of confidence in the truth of appearances is a sign of success, and through continual meditation it can grow stronger and stronger. This process is how you come closer and closer to seeing yourself as you actually are.

Realization of emptiness is difficult, but if you keep working at it—analyzing and analyzing—comprehension definitely will come. You will understand what is meant by searching for inherent existence but not finding it—

searching for what is so strongly imagined and not finding it. This nonfinding appears to the mind as emptiness, first weakly and then with more and more clarity. Though initial insights are not the most profound, as you keep at this process, they will get deeper and deeper.

Through a preliminary sense of emptiness, you will gain a clearer sense of what ignorance is; this will lead to a better experience of emptiness. Knowing emptiness better will, in turn, enhance your identification of ignorance, and what is being negated. This identification will deepen the impact of the reasoning as you use it again and again, inducing more and more understanding and undermining your belief in what is exaggerated. This is how you undo trouble.

17

Extending This Insight to What You Own

Just as you have come to know
The false discrimination of yourself,
Apply this mentally to all phenomena.

—BUDDHA

To review: If there is a concrete "I," then it would have to be either one with mind-body or different from mind-body. Since both of those possibilities are riddled with logical fallacies, you have to come to the conclusion that such a concrete "I" does not exist at all.

It is relatively easy, once you have understood that an inherently existent "I" does not exist, to realize that the sense of inherently existent ownership is mistaken. Mind and body are objects used by that "I." The "I" is like an owner, to whom body and mind belong. Indeed, we say,

"My body is a bit worn down." Or "My body is fit." Such statements are valid. Even though you do not think "This is I" when you look at your arm, when your arm is painful, you definitely do think "I am in pain, I am not well." Still, it is clear that the "I" and the body are different; the body belongs to the "I."

Similarly, we speak of "my mind," and we might say, "My memory is weak; something is wrong." You are the trainer of the mind, which like an unruly student, is going to be taught to do what you want.

In this way, body and mind belong to the "I," and the "I" is their owner. Though it cannot be denied that each performs its respective functions, still there is no independent "I" separate from mind and body that owns these. Your eyes, ears, and so forth are indeed objects that you rightly see as "mine," but they do not exist in the way they so forcefully appear to your mind to be owned by an inherently existent "I." As Nagarjuna says in his *Precious Garland of Advice*:

The Buddha who speaks only to help beings
Said that all beings
Have arisen from the misconception of "I"
And are enveloped with the conception of "mine."

When you realize that the self does not inherently exist, then "mine" could not possibly inherently exist.

Meditative Reflection

Consider:

1. Internal phenomena, such as your mind and your body, belong to you and therefore are "yours."
2. External belongings, such as your clothing or car, also are "yours."
3. If the "I" does not inherently exist, what is "yours" could not possibly inherently exist.

18

Balancing Calm and Insight

Cultivation of meditative stability alone
Will not destroy the discrimination of inherent existence.
Afflictive emotions can return,
Making all sorts of disturbances.

—BUDDHA

Calm abiding can suppress counterproductive emotions, but it cannot totally remove them. Insight is needed because, as explained earlier, it can totally remove troublesome emotions and their consequent embroilments. Stabilizing meditation and analytical meditation must now work together. When they function this way, they can uproot problematic emotions and remove limits on intelligence so that you can fulfill the ultimate goal of helping others more effectively.

The great clarity and stability of calm abiding open the way for analysis to provide truly powerful insight into the emptiness of inherent existence. With direct perception of the emptiness of those phenomena—yourself, other people, and things—that lead you into destructive emotions, problems can be overcome at their root.

To combine calm abiding with special insight, you need to alternate focusing meditation with analytical meditation and bring them into harmony. Too much analysis will promote excitement, making the mind slightly unstable, but too much stability will make you not want to analyze. As the Tibetan sage Tsongkhapa says:

> If you solely perform analytical meditation, the calm abiding generated earlier will degenerate. Therefore, upon having mounted the horse of calm abiding, you should remain within analysis and then periodically alternate this with stabilizing meditation.

UNION OF CALM ABIDING AND SPECIAL INSIGHT

Previously, calm abiding and analysis were like the two ends of a scale, the one becoming slightly lighter when the other became manifest. But now, as you skillfully alternate between stabilizing and analytical meditation, the power of analysis itself induces even greater mental and physical flexibility than before, when calm abiding was achieved by stabilizing meditation. When calm abiding and insight operate in this way, simultaneously with equal power, it is called the "union of calm abiding and special insight." It is also called "wisdom arisen from meditation," as contrasted to the wisdom arisen from hearing, reading, study, or thinking.

Earlier, while reading and thinking about emptiness, your consciousness was aimed at emptiness as an intellectual object of inquiry, so your mind and emptiness were separate and distinct. But now you have the experience of penetrating emptiness without the sense that subject and object are distant from each other. You are approaching a state in which insight and emptiness are like water put into water.

Gradually, the remaining subtle sense of subject and object vanishes, with subject and object entirely merging in total nonconceptuality. As Buddha says, "When the fire of knowing reality just as it is arises from correct analysis itself, the wood of conceptuality is burned, like the fire of sticks rubbed together."

Meditative Reflection

For beginners it is helpful to learn this blueprint for spiritual progress, because it will exert a powerful influence on your development. For the time being, you can alternate a little stabilizing meditation with a little analytical meditation in order both to taste the process and to strengthen your current meditation.

1. First focus your mind on a single object, such as a Buddha image or your breath.
2. Use analytical meditation as described in the four steps for meditating on the nature of the "I." Contemplate the logical impossibility of asserting that the self and mind-body are either the same or different:

ONENESS

- "I" and mind-body would have to be utterly and in all ways one.
- In that case, asserting an "I" would be pointless.
- It would be impossible to think of "my body" or "my head" or "my mind."

- When mind and body no longer exist, the self also would not exist.
- Since mind and body are plural, a person's selves also would be plural.
- Since the "I" is just one, mind and body also would be one.
- Just as mind and body are produced and disintegrate, so it would have to be asserted that the "I" is inherently produced and inherently disintegrates. In this case, neither the pleasurable effects of virtuous actions nor the painful effects of nonvirtuous actions would bear fruit for us, or we would be experiencing the effects of actions we ourselves did not commit.

DIFFERENCE

- "I" and mind-body would have to be completely separate.
- In that case, the "I" would have to be findable after clearing away mind and body.
- The "I" would not have the characteristics of production, abiding, and disintegration, which is absurd.

- The "I" would absurdly have to be just a figment of the imagination or permanent.
- Absurdly, the "I" would not have any physical or mental characteristics.

3. When you develop a little insight, stay with that insight in stabilizing meditation, appreciating its impact.
4. Then, when feeling diminishes a little, return to analytical meditation to reinstate feeling and develop more insight.

Switching back and forth between focusing on a single topic and directed analysis of it will promote deeper experience.

Part V

HOW PERSONS
AND THINGS
ACTUALLY EXIST

19

Viewing Yourself As Like
an Illusion

Like a magician's illusions, dreams,
and a moon reflected in water,
All beings and their environments are empty
of inherent existence.
Though not solidly existent, all these appear
Like water bubbles coming forth in water.

— GUNG TANG

As a result of your having investigated the nature of the
"I" and other phenomena, you now know that they appear
to exist inherently, but you understand that they are
empty of inherent existence, just as an illusion conjured
up by a magician does not exist the way it seems. As Nagarjuna says in his *Precious Garland of Advice*:

A form seen from a distance
Is seen clearly by those nearby.

If a mirage were water,
Why is water not seen by those nearby?

The way this world is seen
As real by those afar
Is not so seen by those nearby,
For whom it is insubstantial, like a mirage.

A face in a mirror appears to be a face, but this image is not a real face in any way; it is from all viewpoints empty of being a face. Likewise, a magician can conjure up illusions that seem to be certain things, like a person in a box being skewered by a sword, but they are not at all established as those things. Similarly, phenomena such as bodies appear to be established from the objects' own side but are empty of being established that way and always have been.

It is not that phenomena *are* illusions; rather, they are *like* illusions. Even if a mirror image of your face is not really your face, the reflection is not utterly nonexistent. Through its appearance you can understand how your actual face looks. Similarly, although persons and things are empty of existing the way they appear to be established in their own right, they are not utterly nonexistent; they can act and can be experienced. Therefore, being like an illusion is not the same as appearing to exist but actually not existing, like the horns of a rabbit, which do not exist at all.

Meditative Reflection

1. Remember a time when you mistook a reflection of a person in a mirror for an actual person.
2. It appeared to be a person but was not.
3. Similarly, all persons and things seem to exist from their own side without depending on causes and conditions, on their parts, and on thought, but they do not.
4. In this way, persons and things are *like* illusions.

IDENTIFYING THE CONFLICT BETWEEN APPEARANCE AND REALITY

I use the examples of illusions, reflections, and mirages in order to provide a rough idea of the conflict between what something appears to be and what it is. Realization that the reflection of a face in a mirror is not a face does not constitute realization of the emptiness of inherent existence of a mirror image, for even with this knowledge you still mistake the nature of a mirror image as inherently existent. If knowing that a mirror image of a face is empty of being a face constituted true realization of emptiness, then as soon as you turned your mind to any other object—your body, your arm, your dwelling—you would also realize its emptiness of inherent existence. But this is not the case. Again, it is not that you and others *are* illusions; rather, you are *like* illusions.

To view yourself or other phenomena as *like* illusions requires two things—the false appearance of objects as inherently existent, and an understanding that you or whatever you are considering does not exist that way. Because of your experience in meditation of searching for and not finding this independent quality (although after meditation, phenomena still *appear* to exist inherently), the power of your previous understanding opens the way for you to recognize that these phenomena are illusory, in that, although they appear to exist inherently, they do not. As Buddha said, "All things have the attribute of falsity, deceptiveness."

There are many discrepancies between the way things appear and the way they really are. Something that is impermanent can appear to be permanent. Also, sources of pain, such as overeating, sometimes appear to be sources of pleasure, but in the end they are not. What will eventually lead to suffering is not seen for what is really is but is mistaken for a way to happiness. Although we want happiness, out of ignorance we do not know how to achieve it; although we do not want pain, because we misunderstand what causes pain, we work at achieving the very causes of pain.

The eyes of those attending a magic show are affected by the magician's tricks, and through this deception, the audience thinks it sees horses, elephants, and so forth. In a similar way, by going along with the appearance of inherent existence, we exaggerate the status of good and bad phenomena, and are thereby led into desire and hatred and actions accumulating karma. What is not an inherently existent "I" appears to be an inherently existent "I," and we accept the appearance as given.

HOW SEEING THIS WAY HELPS

Seeing people and things as existing like illusions helps reduce unfavorable emotions, because lust, hatred, and so forth stem from our superimposing qualities—good or bad—on phenomena beyond what they actually have. For instance, when we get very angry at someone, we have a strong sense of the wretchedness of that person, but later, when we calm down and look at that same person, we may find our earlier perception laughable.

The benefit of insight is that it prevents us from attributing to objects a goodness or badness beyond what is actually there. This undermining of self-deception makes it possible to reduce and eventually end lust and hatred, since these emotions are built on exaggerations. This elimination of unhealthy emotions in turn leaves more room for healthy emotions and virtues to develop. By viewing phenomena with insight, you bring them within the scope of the practice of emptiness.

When you practice expanding love and compassion, keep in mind that love and compassion themselves and the persons who are their objects are like a magician's illusions in that they appear to exist solidly in and of themselves but do not. If you see them as inherently existent, this view will keep you from fully developing love and compassion. Instead, view them as like illusions, existing one way but appearing another. This perspective will deepen both your insight into emptiness and the healthy emotions of love and compassion, so that within such understanding you can engage in effective compassionate activity.

Meditative Reflection

1. As you did earlier, bring the target of your reasoning, the inherently established "I," to mind by remembering or imagining an instance when you strongly believed in it.

2. Notice the ignorance that superimposes inherent existence, and identify it.

3. Put particular emphasis on contemplating the fact that if such inherent establishment exists, the "I" and the mind-body complex would have to be either the same or different.

4. Then forcefully contemplate the absurdity of assertions of the self and mind-body as either the same or different, seeing and feeling the impossibility of those assertions:

ONENESS

- "I" and mind-body would have to be utterly and in all ways one.
- In that case, asserting an "I" would be pointless.
- It would be impossible to think of "my body" or "my head" or "my mind."

- When mind and body no longer exist, the self also would not exist.
- Since mind and body are plural, a person's selves also would be plural.
- Since the "I" is just one, mind and body also would be one.
- Just as mind and body are produced and disintegrate, so it would have to be asserted that the "I" is inherently produced and inherently disintegrates. In this case, neither the pleasurable effects of virtuous actions nor the painful effects of nonvirtuous actions would bear fruit for us, or we would be experiencing the effects of actions we ourselves did not commit.

DIFFERENCE

- "I" and mind-body would have to be completely separate.
- In that case, the "I" would have to be findable after clearing away mind and body.
- The "I" would not have the characteristics of production, abiding, and disintegration, which is absurd.

- The "I" would absurdly have to be just a figment of the imagination or permanent.
- Absurdly, the "I" would not have any physical or mental characteristics.

5. Not finding such an "I," firmly decide, "Neither I nor any person is inherently established."

6. Remain for a while, absorbing the meaning of emptiness, concentrating on the absence of inherent establishment.

7. Then, once again let the appearances of people dawn to your mind.

8. Reflect on the fact that, within the context of dependent-arising, people also engage in actions and thus accumulate karma and experience the effects of those actions.

9. Ascertain the fact that the appearance of people is effective and feasible within the absence of inherent existence.

10. When effectiveness and emptiness seem to be contradictory, use the example of a mirror image:

- The image of a face is undeniably produced in dependence on a face and a mirror, even though it is empty of the eyes, ears, and so forth it appears to have, and the image of a face undeniably disappears when either face or mirror is absent.

- Similarly, although a person does not have even a speck of inherent establishment, it is not contradictory for a person to perform actions, accumulate karma, experience effects, and be born in dependence on karma and destructive emotions.

11. Try to view the lack of contradiction between effectiveness and emptiness with respect to all people and things.

20

Noticing How Everything Depends on Thought

Here even the various mind-pleasing blossoming flowers
And attractive shining supreme golden houses
Have no inherently existent maker at all.
They are set up through the power of thought.
Through the power of conceptuality the world is established.

— BUDDHA

When you develop a rough idea of what it means to be dependent on thought, you should ask yourself whether persons and things usually appear to you this way or not. When we are affected by emotions on a subtle level, it is difficult to identify how we hold on to them. Therefore, consider a time when you felt intense hatred or desire. The hated or desired person or thing seemed extremely substantial, even totally unchanging, didn't it? When you look closely, you will understand that there is no way to claim that you already see phenomena as dependent on thought. You will find that they seem to exist in their own right.

When I was about thirty-five years old, I was reflecting on the meaning of a passage by Tsongkhapa about how the "I" cannot be found either within or separate from the mind-body complex and how the "I" depends for its existence on conceptuality. Here is the passage:

> A coiled rope's speckled color and coiled form are similar to those of a snake, and when the rope is perceived in a dim area, the thought arises, "This is a snake." As for the rope, at that time when it is seen to be a snake, the collection and parts of the rope are not even in the slightest way a snake. Therefore, that snake is merely set up by conceptuality. In the same way, when the thought "I" arises in dependence upon mind and body, nothing within mind and body—neither the collection that is a continuum of earlier and later moments, nor the collection of the parts at one time, nor the separate parts, nor the continuum of any of the separate parts—is in even the slightest way the "I." Also there is not even the slightest something that is a different entity from mind and body that is appre-

hendable as the "I." Consequently, the "I" is *merely* set up by conceptuality in dependence upon mind and body; it is not established by way of its own entity.

Suddenly, it was as if lightning moved through my chest. I was so awestruck that, over the next few weeks, whenever I saw people, they seemed like a magician's illusions in that they appeared to inherently exist but I knew that they actually did not. This is when I began to understand that it is truly possible to stop the process of creating destructive emotions by no longer assenting to the way "I" and other phenomena appear to exist. Every morning I meditate on emptiness, and I recall that experience in order to bring it into the day's activities. Just thinking or saying "I," as in "I will do such-and-such," will often trigger that feeling. But still I cannot claim full understanding of emptiness.

THE MEANING OF BEING SET UP BY CONCEPTUALITY

In the beginning, pretty flowers or a wonderful house appear to exist in and of themselves across from consciousness, but in the end nothing over there is capable of confirming such an existence; rather, the mind's perception is their source. This is the case for all phenomena. When sought, they cannot be found to exist in their own right, despite appearances to the contrary.

It is by way of their helping and harming—which are dependent on consciousness—that they exist. They never did, never do, nor ever will exist from their side, in their own right. They exist through the power of the mind, through the power of conventions.

In the passage cited at the beginning of this chapter, Buddha says that the whole world is dependent on conceptual thinking. Similarly, Aryadeva's *Four Hundred Stanzas on the Yogic Deeds of Bodhisattvas* says:

Since desire and so forth
Do not exist without conceptuality,
Who with intelligence would hold
That these are real objects and are also conceptual?

Chandrakirti's commentary on that stanza indicates that phenomena exist only in the presence of conceptual thought:

Those which exist only when conceptuality exists and do not exist when conceptuality does not are without question definitely not established by way of their own nature, like a snake imagined in a coiled rope.

Exploring the Meaning

How are we to understand the insistence of great Indians and Tibetans on how crucial conceptual thought is? It would be most uncomfortable to hold that, before each and every object comes into our ken, we must have a thought constructing it right at that moment. No matter how fast thought operates, there would not be enough time for all the thoughts that would be needed in a single moment of visual perception.

Indeed, external objects are part of the process of generating consciousness of them, as in the case of seeing a tree and its surroundings, but if dependence on thought meant that a conceptual thought is needed to construct everything we see, this would be absurd. Therefore, it seems to me that, in the end, the meaning of the world's being established by conceptual thought is that objects, without depending on a consciousness, cannot establish their existence right within themselves. From this viewpoint it is said that the world—all phenomena, both persons and things—is set up by conceptual thought.

For instance, it is obvious that effects depend upon

causes, but causes also, in a subtle sense, depend upon effects. Every cause itself is an effect of its own causes, which preceded it, and therefore arises in dependence upon its respective causes. All Buddhist systems assert that effects arise in dependence upon causes. Here cause and effect are in a temporal sequence, an effect occurring after its cause. This is dependent-arising in the sense of *dependent production*.

Only the highest philosophical perspective within Buddhism contains an additional consideration, that because the designation of something as a "cause" depends upon consideration of its effect, in this sense a cause *depends* upon its effect. Something is not a cause in and of itself; it is named a "cause" in relation to its effect. Here the effect does not occur before its cause, and its cause does not come into being after its effect; it is in thinking of its future effect that we designate something as a cause. This is dependent-arising in the sense of *dependent designation*.

As Nagarjuna says in his *Fundamental Treatise on the Middle Called "Wisdom"*:

A doer is dependent on a doing,
And a doing exists dependent on a doer.

Except for dependently arising, we do not see
Another cause for their establishment.

Agent and action depend upon each other. An action is posited in dependence upon an agent, and an agent is posited in dependence upon an action. An action arises in dependence upon an agent, and an agent arises in dependence upon an action. Nevertheless, they are not related in the same way as cause and effect, since the one is not produced before the other.

How is it that, in general, things are relative? How is it that a cause is relative to its effect? It is because it is not established in and of itself. If that were the case, a cause would not need to depend on its effect. But there is no self-sufficient cause, which is why we do not find anything in and of itself when we analytically examine a cause, despite its appearance to our everyday mind that each thing has its own self-contained being. Because things are under the influence of something other than themselves, the designation of something as a cause necessarily depends upon consideration of its effect. This is the route through which we come to realize that this more subtle understanding of dependent-arising as dependent designation is correct.

Recently, while in south India after making a pilgrimage to Mount Shri Parvata, where Nagarjuna lived near the end of his life, I bestowed an initiation on a large audience in a Buddhist tradition called Kalachakra (Wheel of Time). During the initiation, I imparted a transmission of explanation on Tsongkhapa's *Praise of Dependent-Arising* in conjunction with teaching Nagarjuna's *Fundamental Treatise on the Middle Called "Wisdom."* I arrived at the point where Tsongkhapa says:

> When Buddha said, "Whatever depends on
>   conditions
> Is empty of its own inherent existence,"
> What is more amazing
> Than this marvelous advice!

I thought, "This is really so!" What I was thinking is this: Indeed, there might be some animals who know the dependent-arising of cause and effect, but for us humans, the dependent-arising of cause and effect is undeniable. But when you take it further, the dependent-arising of cause and effect comes because of dependent designation, which itself indicates that cause and effect do not have their own being; if they did have their own being, they would not have to be dependently designated. As Nagarjuna's follower Buddhapalita says in commentary on the twenty-second chapter of the *Fundamental Treatise on the Middle Called "Wisdom"*:

> If something exists by way of its own entity, what would be the need for being posited dependently?

Indeed, if a thing existed in itself, that alone would be sufficient. You could just say, "It is this," without needing to relate it to anything else. Because it is not established in and of itself, there is no alternative but to posit it in relation to something else. I have continued to find this thought helpful.

In the same way, Tsongkhapa says in his *Three Principal Aspects of the Path to Enlightenment*:

> With the two realizations of dependent-arising and
>   emptiness existing simultaneously without
>   alternation,
> Definite knowledge entirely destroys the mode of
>   apprehension of inherent existence

Upon only seeing dependent-arising as
  incontrovertible.
At that point analysis of the view of reality is
  complete.

Reflecting on the dependent latticework at the heart of the dependent-arising of cause and effect confirms the understanding that phenomena are merely nominal, merely imputed, and no more than that. When you understand that mere imputation alone undermines the concept that phenomena exist in and of themselves, your task of figuring out the Buddhist view of reality is complete. I have hopes that I am approaching this point.

If you understand that, no matter what appears, whether to your senses or to your thinking mind, those objects are established in dependence upon thought, you will get over the idea that phenomena exist in their own right. You will understand that there is no truth in their being set up from their own side. You will realize emptiness, the absence of inherent existence, which exists beyond the proliferations of problems born from seeing phenomena as existing in themselves and provides the medicine for removing delusion.

Meditative Reflection

1. Revisit a time when you were filled with hatred or desire.
2. Does it not seem that the hated or desired person or thing is extremely substantial, very concrete?
3. Since this is the case, there is no way you can claim that you already see phenomena as dependent on thought.
4. You see them as existing in their own right.
5. Remember that you need frequent meditation on emptiness to counter the false appearance of phenomena.

HOW THIS REALIZATION HELPS IN IDENTIFYING INHERENT EXISTENCE

All Buddhist systems assert that existence and nonexistence are determined by valid cognition. From this perspective, the object and the subject seem to have equal power. The highest Buddhist system, called the Middle Way School, and within it the Consequence School, take this point even further, saying that it is not that a valid consciousness finds things existing in their own right. Rather, those things themselves depend upon being set up by conceptual thought. Nothing can exist except by being set up by conceptuality. Everything is seen to depend on the mind—the mind is the authorizer.

This is why Buddhist scriptures say that the "I" and other phenomena exist only through the power of conceptual thought. Although the "I" is set up in dependence upon mind and body, mind and body are not the "I," nor is the "I" mind and body. There is nothing in the mind and body (in dependence upon which the "I" is set up) that is the "I." Hence, the "I" depends on conceptual thought. It and all other phenomena are only set up by the mind. When you understand this, you get a little idea that persons do not exist in and of themselves and are only dependently established. And when you see that phenomena usually do not seem to be under the influence of conceptuality but seem to exist in their own right, you will think, "Ah! That is what is being refuted."

Meditative Reflection

Consider:

1. The "I" is set up in dependence upon mind and body.
2. However, mind and body are not the "I," nor is the "I" mind and body.

3. Therefore, the "I" depends on conceptual thought, set up by the mind.

4. The fact that the "I" depends on thought implies that the "I" does not exist in and of itself.

5. Now notice that you have a better sense of what it means for something to exist in and of itself, the inherent existence that realization of emptiness is aimed at refuting.

Part VI

DEEPENING LOVE WITH INSIGHT

25

Feeling Empathic

21

Feeling Empathy

Hail to loving concern for transmigrating beings
Powerless like a bucket traveling up and down a well
Through initially exaggerating oneself, "I,"
And then generating attachment for things,
"This is mine."

—CHANDRAKIRTI'S *SUPPLEMENT*

Even though it is necessary in the beginning to have a strong will in order to develop love and compassion, will is not sufficient to develop these altruistic attitudes limitlessly. It is important to join the practice of love and compassion with the practice of insight. Even if you seek to help someone out of concern, without insight you cannot be very clear about what benefit will come of your efforts. A combination is needed: a good human heart as well as a good human brain. With these working together, we can achieve a lot.

A METAPHOR FOR
CONTEMPLATION

In the stanza cited at the beginning of this chapter, Chandrakirti shows how insight can deepen love through understanding the process by which we suffer. He compares the process to the way a bucket moves up and down a well. How are beings born from life to life similar to a bucket in a well? There are six similarities:

1. Just as the bucket is bound by a rope, so beings are constrained by counterproductive emotions and actions driven by them.
2. Just as the movement of the bucket up and down the well is run by an operator, so the process of cyclic existence is run by an untamed mind, specifically through mistakenly believing that a self exists inherently, and then mistaking the nature of "mine."
3. Just as the bucket travels up and down the well over and over, so sentient beings ceaselessly wander in the great well of cyclic existence, from the uppermost states of temporary happiness to the lowest states of temporary pain.
4. Just as it takes great exertion to draw the bucket up

but it descends easily, so beings have to expend great effort to draw themselves upward to a happier life but easily descend into painful situations.

5. Just as a bucket does not determine its own movements, so the factors involved in shaping a person's life are the results of past ignorance, attachment, and grasping; in the present, these same factors are continually creating more problems for our future lives, like waves in the ocean.

6. Just as the bucket bumps against the walls of the well when it ascends and descends, so sentient beings are battered day by day by the suffering of pain and change, and by being caught in processes beyond their control.

Through this simile, Chandrakirti provides insight into the details of the process driving cyclic existence.

First, apply this information about cyclic existence to yourself so that you can understand your own plight and develop a strong intention to transcend this dynamic of recurring problems. If your mind has not been affected by thinking about the way you yourself wander in an uncontrolled cycle of self ruin, then when you reflect on the process of suffering in other sentient beings, you will not find their suffering so unbearable that you would feel the need to help extricate them from this morass.

Meditative Reflection

Consider:

1. Just as a bucket in a well is bound by a rope, so I am constrained by counterproductive emotions and actions driven by them.

2. Just as the movement of a bucket up and down the well is run by an operator, so the process of my cyclic existence is run by my untamed mind, specifically through mistakenly believing that I inherently exist, and that "mine" inherently exists.

3. Just as a bucket travels up and down the well over and over, so I ceaselessly wander in the great well of cyclic existence, from the uppermost states of temporary happiness to the lowest states of temporary pain.

4. Just as it takes great exertion to draw the bucket up but it descends easily, so I have to expend great effort to draw myself upward to a happier life but easily descend to painful situations.

5. Just as a bucket does not determine its own movements, so the factors involved in shaping my life are

the results of past ignorance, attachment, and grasping; in the present, these same factors are continually creating more problems for my future lives, like waves in the ocean.

6. Just as a bucket bumps against the walls of the well when it ascends and descends, so I am battered day by day by the suffering of pain and change, and by being caught in processes beyond my control.

7. Therefore, from the depths of my heart I should seek to get out of this cyclic round of suffering.

Extending This Insight to Others

Now that you have identified the mechanics of misery in your own situation, you can extend this insight to other sentient beings suffering the same miseries. However, for your response to be love and compassion, it is not sufficient just to know how other beings suffer; you must also have a sense of closeness with them. Otherwise, the more you know about your enemies' suffering, the happier you might be! As Tsongkhapa says:

> In the world when suffering is seen in an enemy, not only is it not unbearable but you delight in it. When persons who have neither helped nor harmed

you are seen to suffer, you will in most cases pay no attention to their situation. This reaction is caused by not having a sense of closeness with respect to those persons. But when you see friends suffer, it is unbearable [in the sense that you want to do something about it], and the degree of unbearability is just as great as your sense of closeness to them. Therefore, it is essential that you generate a sense of strong cherishing and affection for sentient beings.

True love and compassion rise on the basis of respecting others. This feeling of empathy is achieved by recognizing that you and all others—whether friends, enemies, or neutral parties—share a central aspiration by wanting happiness and not wanting suffering, even if you view happiness and suffering differently. Also, it helps to be aware that, over the course of countless lifetimes, everyone at some time has been your mother and your closest friend. (I have explained these points in detail in *How to Expand Love.*)

With this prerequisite sense of closeness and intimacy with everyone in place, insight into how sentient beings wander powerlessly in cyclic existence serves to heighten love and compassion. In the presence of intimacy and insight, the factors of love, compassion, and a desire to help others arise without difficulty.

Meditative Reflection

Bring a friend to mind, and cultivate three levels of love:

1. This person wants happiness but is bereft. How nice it would be if she or he could be imbued with happiness and all the causes of happiness!

2. This person wants happiness but is bereft. May she or he be imbued with happiness and all the causes of happiness!

3. This person wants happiness but is bereft. I will do whatever I can to help her or him to be imbued with happiness and all the causes of happiness!

Now cultivate three levels of compassion:

1. This person wants happiness and does not want suffering, yet is stricken with terrible pain. If this person could only be free from suffering and the causes of suffering!

2. This person wants happiness and does not want suffering, yet is stricken with terrible pain. May this

person be free from suffering and the causes of suffering!

3. This person wants happiness and does not want suffering, yet is stricken with terrible pain. I will help this person be free from suffering and all the causes of suffering!

Now cultivate total commitment:

1. Cyclic existence is a process driven by ignorance.
2. Therefore, it is realistic for me to work to achieve enlightenment and to help others do the same.
3. Even if I have to do it alone, I will free all sentient beings from suffering and the causes of suffering, and set all sentient beings in happiness and its causes.

One by one, bring to mind individual beings—first friends, then neutral persons, and then enemies, starting with the least offensive—and repeat these reflections with them. It will take months and years, but the benefit of this practice will be immense.

22

Reflecting on Impermanence

In Tibet there were practitioners in retreat
who so strongly reflected on impermanence
that they would not wash their dishes after supper.

—PALTRUL RINPOCHE'S *SACRED WORD*

In this chapter I will explain impermanence, the first of
two deeper levels of insight into the process of cyclic existence. The second, emptiness, will be treated in the next
chapter.

A METAPHOR
FOR IMPERMANENCE

A reflection of the moon shimmers on the surface of a lake
rippled by breezes. A huge river of the ignorance that mistakenly believes the mind-body to be inherently existent
flows into the lake of mistaking "I" as inherently existent.

The lake itself is agitated by the winds of counterproductive thought and of wholesome and unwholesome actions. The shimmering reflection of the moon symbolizes both the coarse level of impermanence, due to death, and the subtle level of impermanence, due to the moment-by-moment disintegration that rules sentient beings. The shining of the rippling waves illustrates the impermanence to which sentient beings are subject, and you are to see sentient beings this way. By reflecting on this metaphor, you can develop insight into how beings are unnecessarily drawn into suffering by being out of tune with their own nature; this insight, in turn, stimulates love and compassion.

REALIZING IMPERMANENCE

We are under the influence of an illusion of permanence, so we think there is always lots of time remaining. This mistaken belief puts us in great danger of wasting our lives in procrastination, which is especially wasteful when our lives are blessed with the leisure and facilities to engage in productive practices. To counteract this tendency, it is important to meditate on impermanence—first on the fact that death might come at any moment, and then on the very momentary nature of our lives.

One of the chief reasons desire and hatred arise is that we are overly attached to the current flow of life. We have a sense that it will last forever, and with that sort of attitude we become fixated on superficialities—material possessions and temporary friends and situations. To overcome this ignorance, you need to reflect on the fact that a day is coming when you will not be here.

Even though there is no certainty that you will die tonight, when you cultivate an awareness of death, you appreciate that you *could* die tonight. With this attitude, if there is something you can do that will help in both this life and the next, you will give it precedence over something that would help only this life in a superficial way. Furthermore, by being uncertain about when death will come, you will refrain from doing something that would harm both your present and your future lifetimes. You will be motivated to develop outlooks that act as antidotes to the various forms of untamed mind. Then, whether you live a day, a week, a month, or a year, that time will be meaningful, because your thoughts and actions will be based on what is beneficial in the long run. By contrast, when you come under the influence of the illusion of permanence and spend your time on matters that go no deeper than the surface of this life, you sustain great loss.

The fact that things change from moment to moment opens up the possibility for positive development. If situations did not change, they would forever retain their aspect of suffering. Once you realize things are always changing, if you are passing through a difficult period you can find comfort in knowing that the situation will not remain that way forever.

It is the nature of cyclic existence that what has gathered—parents, children, brothers, sisters, and friends—will eventually disperse. No matter how much friends like each other, eventually they must separate. Gurus and students, parents and children, brothers and sisters, husbands and wives, and the very best of friends—no matter who they are—must eventually separate. In addition to separating from all of our friends, all the wealth and resources you have accumulated—no matter how marvelous they are—eventually become unusable; the brevity of this present life will force you to leave all wealth behind. The Indian philosopher and yogi Shantideva speaks evocatively of impermanence, saying that, no matter how wonderful your present life comes to be, it is like dreaming about pleasure and then being awakened, with nothing left except memory. As Buddha says in the *Diamond Cutter Sutra*:

> View things compounded from causes
> To be like twinkling stars, figments seen with an eye
>   disease,
> The flickering light of a butter-lamp, magical
>   illusions,
> Dew, bubbles, dreams, lightning, and clouds.

When I am about to start a lecture in front of a large crowd of people looking up to me for wisdom and insight, I repeat to myself these lines about the fragility of everything and then snap my fingers, the brief sound symbolizing impermanence. This is how I remind myself that I will soon be descending from my current position. Any living being—no matter how long he or she lives—must eventually die. There is no other way. Once you dwell within cyclic existence, you cannot live outside its nature. No matter how marvelous things may be, it is built into their very nature that they and you must degenerate in the end. As Buddha said, "Realize that the body is impermanent like a clay vessel."

Good fortune is not permanent; consequently, it is dangerous to become too attached to things going well. Any outlook of permanence is ruinous. When the present becomes your preoccupation, the future does not matter, which undermines your motivation to engage in compassionate practices for the future enlightenment of others. By contrast, an outlook of impermanence provides the proper motivation.

Not only must you die in the end but you do not know when the end will come. You should make preparations so that, even if you did die tonight, you would have no regrets. If you develop an appreciation for the imminence of death, your sense of the importance of using time wisely will get stronger and stronger. As Nagarjuna's *Precious Garland of Advice* says:

> You are living amidst the causes of death
> Like a lamp standing in a breeze.
> Having let go of all possessions,
> At death powerless you must go elsewhere,
> But all that has been used for spiritual practice
> Will precede you as good karma.

If you keep in mind how quickly this life disappears, you will value your time and do what is most helpful. With a strong sense of the imminence of death, you will feel the need to engage in spiritual practice, improving your mind and not wasting your time on various distractions ranging from eating and drinking to endless talk about war, romance, and gossip.

For one who cannot face even the word *death,* never mind the reality of it, the actual arrival of death is likely to bring great discomfort and fear. But those who are accustomed to reflecting on the imminence of death are prepared to face death with no regret. Reflecting on the uncertainty of the time of death develops a mind that is peaceful, disciplined, and virtuous, because it is dwelling on more than the superficial stuff of this short lifetime.

We all share an existence marked by suffering and impermanence. Once we recognize how much we have in common, we see that there is no sense in being belligerent with one another. Consider a group of prisoners who are about to be executed. Over the course of their stay together in prison, all of them will meet their end. There is no sense in quarreling during their remaining days. Like those prisoners, all of us are bound by suffering and impermanence. Under such circumstances, there is absolutely no reason to fight with one another or to waste all our energy, mental as well as physical, on accumulating money and property.

Meditative Reflection

Take this to heart:

1. It is certain that I will die. Death cannot be avoided. My life span is running out and cannot be extended.
2. When I will die is indefinite. Life spans among humans vary. The causes of death are many, and the causes of life comparatively few. The body is fragile.
3. At death nothing will help except my transformed attitude. Friends will be of no help. My wealth will be of no use, and neither will my body.
4. We are all in this same perilous situation, so there is no point in quarreling and fighting or wasting all our mental and physical energy on accumulating money and property.
5. I should practice now to reduce my attachment to passing fancies.
6. From the depths of my heart I should seek to get beyond this cycle of suffering induced by misconceiving the impermanent to be permanent.

SUBTLE IMPERMANENCE

The substances that make up the objects around us disintegrate moment by moment; similarly, the internal consciousness with which we observe those external objects also disintegrates moment by moment. This is the nature of subtle impermanence. Particle physicists do not just take for granted the appearance of a solid object such as a table; instead they look at changes within its smaller elements.

Ordinary happiness is like the dew on the tip of a blade of grass, disappearing very quickly. That it vanishes reveals that it is impermanent and under the control of other forces, causes, and conditions. Its vanishing also shows that there is no way of making everything right; no matter what you do within the scope of cyclic existence, you cannot pass beyond the range of suffering. By seeing that the true nature of things is impermanence, you will not be shocked by change when it occurs, not even by death.

Meditative Reflection

Consider:

1. My mind, body, possessions, and life are impermanent simply because they are produced by causes and conditions.

2. The very same causes that produce my mind, body, possessions, and life also make them disintegrate moment by moment.

3. The fact that things have a nature of impermanence indicates that they are not under their own power; they function under outside influence.

4. By mistaking what disintegrates moment by moment for something constant, I bring pain upon myself as well as others.

5. From the depths of my heart I should seek to get beyond this round of suffering induced by mistaking the impermanent to be permanent.

EXTENDING THIS TO OTHERS

Since our attitudes of permanence and self-cherishing are what ruin all of us, the most fruitful meditations are on impermanence and the emptiness of inherent existence on the one hand and love and compassion on the other. This is why Buddha emphasized that the two wings of the bird flying to enlightenment are compassion and wisdom.

Extrapolating from your own experience of not recognizing the impermanent for what it actually is, you can appreciate how it is that other sentient beings wander through limitless forms of cyclic existence by making the same mistake. Contemplate their inconceivable suffering and their similarity to you in wanting happiness and not wanting suffering. Over the course of innumerable lifetimes, they have been your closest friends, sustaining you with kindness, which makes them intimates. Seeing that you have a responsibility to help them possess happiness and to help free them from suffering, develop great love and great compassion.

Sometimes when I am visiting a big city, staying on a high floor in a hotel, I look down on the traffic, hundreds and even thousands of cars going this way and that, and reflect that, although all these beings are impermanent, they are thinking, "I want to be happy," "I must do this job," "I must get this money," "I have to do this." They are mistakenly imagining themselves to be permanent. This thought stimulates my compassion.

Meditative Reflection

Bring a friend to mind and consider the following with feeling:

1. This person's mind, body, possessions, and life are impermanent because they are produced by causes and conditions.
2. The very same causes that produce this person's mind, body, possessions, and life also make them disintegrate moment by moment.
3. The fact that things have a nature of impermanence indicates that they are not under their own power; they function under outside influence.
4. By mistaking what disintegrates moment by moment for something constant, this friend brings pain upon himself or herself as well as others.

Now cultivate three levels of love:

1. This person wants happiness but is bereft. How nice it would be if she or he could be imbued with happiness and all the causes of happiness!
2. This person wants happiness but is bereft. May she or

he be imbued with happiness and all the causes of happiness!

3. This person wants happiness but is bereft. I will do whatever I can to help her or him to be imbued with happiness and all the causes of happiness!

Now cultivate three levels of compassion:

1. This person wants happiness and does not want suffering, yet is stricken with terrible pain. If this person could only be free from suffering and the causes of suffering!

2. This person wants happiness and does not want suffering, yet is stricken with terrible pain. May this person be free from suffering and the causes of suffering!

3. This person wants happiness and does not want suffering, yet is stricken with terrible pain. I will help this person be free from suffering and all the causes of suffering!

Now cultivate total commitment:

1. Cyclic existence is a process driven by ignorance.
2. Therefore, it is realistic for me to work to achieve enlightenment and to help others do the same.

3. Even if I have to do it alone, I will free all sentient beings from suffering and the causes of suffering, and set all sentient beings in happiness and its causes.

One by one, bring to mind individual beings—first friends, then neutral persons, and then enemies, starting with the least offensive—and repeat these reflections with them. It will take months and years, but the benefit will be vast.

Absorbing Yourself in Ultimate Love

It is not sufficient that the doctrine be great.
The person must have a great attitude.
—TIBETAN SAYING

Now we turn to the most profound level of love and compassion, which is made possible by knowledge of the emptiness of inherent existence. Chandrakirti puts it this way:

> I offer homage to loving concern viewing trans-migrators as empty of inherent existence though they appear to exist inherently, like a reflection of the moon in water.

The reflection of the moon in clear, calm water appears to be the moon in every respect but is not the moon in any respect, which is actually in the sky. This image symbolizes the appearance of "I" and all other phenomena as if they inherently exist: though appearing to exist in their own right, they are empty of such. Like someone mistaking a reflection of the moon for the moon, we mistake the appearance of "I" and other phenomena for things that exist in their own right.

You can use this metaphor as a way to develop insight into how we are unnecessarily drawn into suffering by assenting to false appearances, thereby falling prey to lust and hatred and all the actions that stem from them, accumulating karma, and being born over and over again in a cycle of pain. This insight will stimulate profound love and compassion because you will vividly see how unnecessary all these ills are.

Here sentient beings are seen not only as suffering in a sixfold process like a bucket in a well, and as imbued with momentary impermanence like a shimmering reflection, but also as subject to the ignorance of going along with the false appearance of inherent existence. With this insight fresh in your mind, great love and great compassion arise in you for all sentient beings; you feel close to them because they want happiness and not suffering just as you do, and you feel the impact of their having been your closest friends over the course of countless lifetimes, sustaining you with kindness.

To gain access to this depth of love and compassion, it is necessary first to understand that you yourself and other sentient beings are empty of inherent existence. Therefore, let us review the steps for realizing the final nature of "I."

Meditative Reflection

1. As you did earlier, bring the target of your reasoning, the inherently established "I," to mind by remembering or imagining an instance when you strongly believed in it.

2. Notice the ignorance that superimposes inherent existence, and identify it.

3. Put particular emphasis on contemplating the fact that if such inherent establishment exists, the "I" and the mind-body complex would have to be either the same or different.

4. Then forcefully contemplate the absurdity of assertions of the self and mind-body as either the same or different, seeing and feeling the impossibility of those assertions:

ONENESS

- "I" and mind-body would have to be utterly and in all ways one.
- In that case, asserting an "I" would be pointless.
- It would be impossible to think of "my body" or "my head" or "my mind."
- When mind and body no longer exist, the self also would not exist.
- Since mind and body are plural, a person's selves also would be plural.
- Since the "I" is just one, mind and body also would be one.
- Just as mind and body are produced and disintegrate, so it would have to be asserted that the "I" is inherently produced and inherently disintegrates. In this case, neither the pleasurable effects of virtuous actions nor the painful effects of non-virtuous actions would bear fruit for us, or we would be experiencing the effects of actions we ourselves did not commit.

DIFFERENCE

- "I" and mind-body would have to be completely separate.
- In that case, the "I" would have to be findable after clearing away mind and body.
- The "I" would not have the characteristics of production, abiding, and disintegration, which is absurd.
- The "I" would absurdly have to be just a figment of the imagination or permanent.
- Absurdly, the "I" would not have any physical or mental characteristics.

5. Not finding such an "I," firmly decide, "Neither I nor any person is inherently established."

6. Resolve: From the depths of my heart I should seek to get beyond this round of suffering brought on myself by misconceiving what does not inherently exist as inherently existing.

EXTENDING THIS TO OTHERS

Destructive attitudes are our internal enemies, the basis for all problems. How are they produced? From lust and hatred, whose root is ignorance. Since these afflictive emotions cause only harm and never help, they must be overcome. In order to do so we must deal with their causes.

All problematic emotions derive from the basic destructive emotion, an ignorant consciousness that both does not know how persons and things actually are and actively misconstrues their nature. We should see destructive emotions as enemies, first identifying them and then engaging in techniques to destroy them.

Driven by afflictive emotions, we engage in actions that establish counterproductive tendencies in the mind. Nonvirtuous actions result in rebirth in unhappier lives, and virtuous actions result in rebirth in happier lives. Both stem from vast ignorance, however. Through directly realizing the truth—the emptiness of inherent existence—and becoming accustomed to it in meditation, you will stop accumulating karma that drives your rebirth in cyclic existence; rebirth will come under your own power to direct it in order to help others more effectively.

Since cyclic existence is rooted in the misapprehension of inherent existence, the only way out of cyclic existence is recognizing this fallacy for what it is. Though there are many factors producing cyclic existence, only at its root—ignorance—can it be severed, for this is the source of all the other causes. Through the meditative reflections in this book, you have learned how to cultivate antidotes to those causes in order to put an end to suffering and the causes of suffering. When you internalize this process, you generate an intention to achieve liberation with more than just words.

Through practice, your aims become transformed; you generate a heartfelt intention to leave the round of pain, at which point you become a spiritual practitioner of increased capacity. As the Tibetan scholar-yogi Tsongkhapa tells us in his *Three Principal Aspects of the Path to Enlightenment,* at this point you focus night and day on attaining liberation: You are intent on relief. From the depths of your mind, you have decided that if you do not attain liberation from the entire process of cyclic existence, the value of your human lifetime will not have been fulfilled.

Being a human is the best possible basis for achieving liberation from cyclic existence, for using the three practices of morality, concentrated meditation, and wisdom.

The practice of morality involves restraining overtly poor behavior of body, speech, and mind. More subtle ill behaviors are suppressed through training in the concentrated meditation of calm abiding. The final abandonment of ill deeds is achieved through training in the wisdom of insight into the emptiness of inherent existence.

Initially, you train in morality because, when you function under the influence of gross afflictive emotions, your physical and verbal behavior becomes harsh, harming yourself and others. Morality involves controlling these gross activities so that they do not manifest; however, the practice of morality cannot eradicate afflictive emotions. And only when afflictive emotions are completely extinguished will you attain liberation.

This is the procedure you should undertake once you understand your plight in cyclic existence:

1. First, train in recognizing the extent of suffering in this life.
2. Then, generate distaste for all forms of the round of suffering from one life to another, called "cyclic existence," and train in morality, concentrated meditation, and wisdom.
3. Eventually, through fully accomplishing these prac-

tices, you can attain a state of liberation from cyclic existence in which suffering has been completely extinguished.

In this way you can achieve liberation, but even then your own aims will not have been brought to complete fulfillment. You still have not overcome the primary obstacle to a full ability to help others: predispositions left in the mind by ignorance of the true nature of persons and things. Even though ignorance itself has been overcome, these predispositions lie latent in the mind, keeping it from knowing all that can be known.

While you are in this state, even if you try to help others, no more than a little benefit can be accomplished. Although it is unquestionably beneficial to achieve liberation from cyclic existence, in terms of quality of mind, your outlook is still involved primarily with your own welfare. In terms of your own progress, the process of overcoming obstructions and realizing high states is not yet complete; you are still dwelling in a form of solitary peace.

It is important not to become inclined toward solitary peace, because by aiming merely at liberation for your own sake, you lengthen the process of attaining altruistic enlightenment directed to others' good—the ultimate goal.

By mainly taking care of yourself, you foster a self-cherishing attitude, and this attitude is difficult to overcome later, when you train in great love and great compassion. Consequently, it is crucial from the very beginning not to fully invest your strength of mind in your own benefit.

By understanding emptiness, you realize that it is possible to break free from your own entrapment in cyclic existence, which makes firm your resolve to leave cyclic existence; when you understand that the suffering of others is also induced by ignorance, you realize that it is possible for them to free themselves from all suffering, strengthening your decision to help others. In this way, insight makes love and compassion realistic expressions of deep knowledge. As Buddha said, "The Buddha's compassion for sentient beings is generated through contemplating, 'Whereas all phenomena are empty, sentient beings cling to views of inherent existence.'"

Understanding that beings are empty of inherent existence, you develop even more profound love and compassion by holistically seeing how they bring suffering on themselves through ignorance of the nature of people and other phenomena. Realizing the emptiness of inherent existence opens the way to enhance love and compassion.

Understanding the ultimate nature of persons and things calls to mind limitless sentient beings who are similar to you in wanting happiness and not wanting suffering, who over the course of countless lifetimes have been your closest friends, sustaining you with kindness. From this sense of intimacy combined with knowledge of why they suffer cyclic rounds of pain through rebirth, you call forth powerful concern for their well-being.

Meditative Reflection

Bring a friend to mind and, while remembering the process of self-ruinous cyclic existence, consider the following:

1. Like me, this person is lost in an ocean of misapprehension of "I" as inherently existent, fed by a huge river of ignorance mistaking mind and body to be inherently existent, and agitated by winds of counterproductive thoughts and actions.

2. Like someone mistaking a reflection of the moon in water for the moon itself, this person mistakes the appearance of "I" and other phenomena to mean they exist in their own right.

3. By accepting this false appearance, this person is pow-

erlessly drawn into lust and hatred, accumulating karma and being born over and over again in a round of pain.

4. Through this process this person unnecessarily brings pain upon himself or herself as well as others.

Now cultivate three levels of love:

1. This person wants happiness but is bereft. How nice it would be if she or he could be imbued with happiness and all the causes of happiness!

2. This person wants happiness but is bereft. May she or he be imbued with happiness and all the causes of happiness!

3. This person wants happiness but is bereft. I will do whatever I can to help her or him to be imbued with happiness and all the causes of happiness!

Now cultivate three levels of compassion:

1. This person wants happiness and does not want suffering, yet is stricken with terrible pain. If this person could only be free from suffering and the causes of suffering!

2. This person wants happiness and does not want suffering, yet is stricken with terrible pain. May this person be free from suffering and the causes of suffering!

3. This person wants happiness and does not want suffering, yet is stricken with terrible pain. I will help this person be free from suffering and all the causes of suffering!

Now cultivate total commitment:

1. Cyclic existence is a process driven by ignorance.
2. Therefore, it is realistic for me to work to achieve enlightenment and to help others do the same.
3. Even if I have to do it alone, I will free all sentient beings from suffering and the causes of suffering, and set all sentient beings in happiness and its causes.

One by one, bring to mind individual sentient beings—first friends, then neutral persons, and then enemies, starting with the least offensive—and repeat these reflections with them. It will take months and years, but the benefit of this practice will be extraordinary.

THE IMPACT OF GREAT LOVE
AND COMPASSION

Be willing to familiarize yourself with this attitude, taking on yourself the burden of protecting all sentient beings from all problems; do it repeatedly and with regular analysis. Your empathy will be so great that it will suffuse your entire being. Without any desire for reward, your aim will be solely the development of others, never disheartened or discouraged in your task.

APPENDIX:

Reviewing the
Meditative Reflections

Part I. The Need for Insight

I. LAYING THE GROUND FOR INSIGHT TO GROW

1. All counterproductive emotions are based on and depend upon ignorance of the true nature of persons and things.

2. There are specific ways to suppress lust and hatred temporarily, but if we undermine the ignorance that misconceives the nature of ourselves, others, and all things, all destructive emotions are undermined.

3. Ignorance sees phenomena—which actually do not exist in and of themselves—as existing independent of thought.

2. DISCOVERING THE SOURCE OF PROBLEMS

Consider:

1. Does the attractiveness of an object seem to be integral to it?

2. Does the attractiveness of an object obscure its faults and disadvantages?

3. Does exaggeration of the pleasantness of certain objects lead to lust?

4. Does exaggeration of the unpleasantness of certain objects lead to hatred?

5. Notice how you:

   - First perceive an object
   - Then notice if the object is good or bad
   - Then conclude that the object has its own independent basis for existing
   - Then conclude that the object's goodness or badness exists inherently in the object
   - Then generate lust or hatred according to your previous judgment.

3. WHY UNDERSTANDING THE TRUTH IS NEEDED

Consider this:

1. Ignorance leads to exaggerating the importance of beauty, ugliness, and other qualities.

2. Exaggeration of these qualities leads to lust, hatred, jealousy, belligerence, and so on.

3. These destructive emotions lead to actions contaminated by misperception.

4. These actions (karma) lead to powerless birth and re-birth in cyclic existence and repeated entanglement in trouble.

5. Removing ignorance undermines our exaggeration of positive and negative qualities; this undercuts lust, ha-tred, jealousy, belligerence, and so on, putting an end to actions contaminated by misperception, thereby ceasing powerless birth and rebirth in cyclic existence.

6. Insight is the way out.

Part II. How to Undermine Ignorance

4. FEELING THE IMPACT OF INTERRELATEDNESS

1. Bring to mind an impermanent phenomenon, such as a house.

2. Consider its coming into being in dependence upon specific causes: lumber, carpenters, and so forth.

3. See if this dependence conflicts with the phenome-non's appearance of existing in its own right.

Then:

1. Bring to mind an impermanent phenomenon, such as a book.

2. Consider its coming into being in dependence upon its parts—its pages and cover.

3. See if its dependence upon its parts conflicts with its appearing as if it exists in its own right.

Then:

1. Consider consciousness paying attention to a blue vase.
2. Reflect on its coming into being in dependence upon its parts—the several moments that constitute its continuum.
3. See if its dependence upon its parts conflicts with its appearing as if it exists in its own right.

Then:

1. Consider space in general.
2. Reflect on its coming into being in dependence upon its parts—north, south, east, and west.
3. See if its dependence upon its parts conflicts with its appearing as if it exists in its own right.

Also:

1. Consider the space of a cup.
2. Reflect on its coming into being in dependence upon its parts—the top half and the bottom half of the cup.

3. See if its dependence upon its parts conflicts with its appearing as if it exists in its own right.

5. APPRECIATING THE REASONING OF DEPENDENT-ARISING

Consider:

1. Dependent and independent are a dichotomy. Anything that exists is either the one or the other.
2. When something is dependent, it must be empty of being under its own power.
3. Nowhere in the parts of the body and mind that form the basis for the "I" can we find the "I." Therefore, the "I" is established not under its own power but through the force of other conditions—its causes, its parts, and thought.

6. SEEING THE INTERDEPENDENCE OF PHENOMENA

Consider:

1. Inherent existence never did, never does, and never will exist.
2. However, we imagine that it does exist and thereby are drawn into distressing emotions.

3. The belief that phenomena inherently exist is an extreme of exaggeration, a frightful chasm.

4. The belief that impermanent phenomena cannot perform functions, or act as cause and effect, is an extreme form of denial, another frightful chasm.

5. The realization that all phenomena are empty of inherent existence because of being dependent-arisings avoids both extremes. Realizing that phenomena are dependent-arisings avoids the extreme of dangerous denial; realizing that they are empty of inherent existence avoids the extreme of dangerous exaggeration.

7. VALUING DEPENDENT-ARISING AND EMPTINESS

Consider:

1. Because persons and things are dependent-arisings, they are empty of inherent existence. Being dependent, they are not self-instituting.

2. Because persons and things are empty of inherent existence, they must be dependent-arisings. If phenomena did exist in their own right, they could not depend on other factors: either causes, their own parts,

or thought. Since phenomena are not able to set themselves up, they can transform.

3. These two realizations should work together, the one furthering the other.

Part III. Harnessing the Power of Concentration and Insight

8. FOCUSING YOUR MIND

1. Look carefully at an image of Buddha, or some other religious figure or symbol, noticing its form, color, and details.

2. Work at causing this image to appear internally to your consciousness, imagining it on the same level as your eyebrows, about five or six feet in front of you, about one to four inches high (smaller is better), and shining brightly.

3. Consider the image to be real, endowed with magnificent qualities of body, speech, and mind.

9. TUNING YOUR MIND FOR MEDITATION

1. Place your mind on the object of meditation.

2. Using introspection, from time to time check to see whether your mind remains on the object.

3. When you find that it has strayed, recall the object and put your mind back on it as often as needed.

Then:

1. To counter laxity, which is a too-loose way of perceiving the meditative object:
   - First try to tighten just a little your way of holding the object.
   - If that does not work, brighten or elevate the object or pay closer attention to its details.
   - If that does not work, leave the intended object and temporarily think about a joyous topic, such as the marvelous qualities of love and compassion or the wonderful opportunity that a human lifetime affords for spiritual practice.
   - If that does not work, leave off meditating and go to a high place or one where there is a vast view.

2. To counter excitement, which is a too-tight way of perceiving the meditative object:
   - First try to loosen just a little your way of imagining the object.
   - If that does not work, lower the object in your mind and imagine it as heavier.

- If that does not work, leave the intended object and temporarily think about a topic that makes you more sober, such as how ignorance brings about the sufferings of cyclic existence, or the imminence of death, or the disadvantages of the object to which you have strayed and the disadvantages of distraction itself.

Part IV. How to End Self-Deception

10. MEDITATING ON YOURSELF FIRST

Consider:

1. The person is at the center of all troubles.
2. Therefore, it is best to work at understanding your true nature first.
3. After that, this realization can be applied to mind, body, house, car, money, and all other phenomena.

11. REALIZING THAT YOU DO NOT EXIST IN AND OF YOURSELF

1. Imagine that someone else criticizes you for something you actually have not done, pointing a finger at you and saying, "You ruined such-and-such."

2. Watch your reaction. How does the "I" appear to your mind?

3. In what way are you apprehending it?

4. Notice how that "I" seems to stand by itself, self-instituting, established by way of its own character.

Also:

1. Remember a time when you were fed up with your mind, such as when you failed to remember something.

2. Review your feelings. How did the "I" appear to your mind at that time?

3. In what way were you apprehending it?

4. Notice how that "I" seems to stand by itself, self-instituting, established by way of its own character.

Also:

1. Remember a time when you were fed up with your body, or with some feature of your body, such as your hair.

2. Look at your feelings. How did the "I" appear to your mind at that time?

3. In what way were you apprehending it?

4. Notice how that "I" seems to stand by itself, self-instituting, established by way of its own character.

Also:

1. Remember a time when you did something awful and you thought, "I really made a mess of things."
2. Consider your feelings. How did the "I" appear to your mind at that time?
3. In what way were you apprehending it?
4. Notice how that "I" seems to stand by itself, self-instituting, established by way of its own character.

Also:

1. Remember a time when you did something wonderful and you took great pride in it.
2. Examine your feelings. How did the "I" appear to your mind at that time?
3. In what way were you apprehending it?
4. Notice how that "I" seems to stand by itself, self-instituting, established by way of its own character.

Also:

1. Remember a time when something wonderful happened to you and you took great pleasure in it.
2. Watch your feelings. How did the "I" appear to your mind at that time?

3. In what way were you apprehending it?

4. Notice how that "I" seems to stand by itself, self-instituting, established by way of its own character.

12. DETERMINING THE CHOICES

1. Analyze whether the "I" that is inherently self-established in the context of the mind-body complex could have a way of existing other than being part of or separate from mind and body.

2. Take other phenomena, such as a cup and a table, or a house and a mountain, as examples. See that there is no third category of existence. They are either the same or different.

3. Decide that if the "I" inherently exists as it seems to, it must be either one with or separate from mind and body.

13. ANALYZING ONENESS

Consider the consequences if the "I" is established in and of itself in accordance with how it appears to our minds and if it also is the same as mind-body:

1. "I" and mind-body would have to be utterly and in all ways one.

2. In that case, asserting an "I" would be pointless.
3. It would be impossible to think of "my body" or "my head" or "my mind."
4. When mind and body no longer exist, the self also would not exist.
5. Since mind and body are plural, one person's selves also would be plural.
6. Since the "I" is just one, mind and body also would be one.
7. Just as mind and body are produced and disintegrate, so it would have to be asserted that the "I" is inherently produced and inherently disintegrates. In this case, neither the pleasurable effects of virtuous actions nor the painful effects of nonvirtuous actions would bear fruit for us, or we would be experiencing the effects of actions we ourselves did not commit.

14. ANALYZING DIFFERENCE

Consider the consequences if the "I" is established in and of itself in accordance with how it appears to our minds and if it also is inherently different from mind body:

1. "I" and mind-body would have to be completely separate.

2. In that case, the "I" would have to be findable after clearing away mind and body.

3. The "I" would not have the characteristics of production, abiding, and disintegration, which is absurd.

4. The "I" would absurdly have to be just a figment of the imagination or permanent.

5. Absurdly, the "I" would not have any physical or mental characteristics.

15. COMING TO A CONCLUSION

Repeatedly review the four steps to realization:

1. Zero in on the target, the appearance of the "I" as if it is established in and of itself.

2. Determine that if the "I" exists the way it seems to, it must be either one with mind and body or separate from mind and body.

3. Thoroughly contemplate the problems with "I" and the mind-body complex being the same.

   - "I" and mind-body would have to be utterly and in all ways one.

   - Asserting an "I" would be pointless.

   - It would be impossible to think of "my body" or "my head" or "my mind."

- When mind and body no longer exist, the self also would not exist.
- Since mind and body are plural, a person's selves also would be plural.
- Since the "I" is just one, mind and body also would be one.
- Just as mind and body are produced and disintegrate, the "I" is inherently produced and inherently disintegrates. In this case, neither the pleasurable effects of virtuous actions nor the painful effects of nonvirtuous actions would bear fruit for us, or we would be experiencing the effects of actions we ourselves did not commit.

4. Thoroughly contemplate the problems with "I" and the mind-body complex being inherently different.
- "I" and mind-body would have to be completely separate.
- In that case, the "I" would have to be findable after clearing away mind and body.
- The "I" would not have the characteristics of production, abiding, and disintegration, which is absurd.
- The "I" would absurdly have to be just a figment of the imagination or permanent.

- Absurdly, the "I" would not have any physical or mental characteristics.

16. Testing Your Realization

1. Go through the four steps of analysis described in Chapter 15.
2. When the sense that the "I" is self-instituting falls apart and vanishes in a void, switch to considering your arm, for instance.
3. See whether the sense that your arm inherently exists immediately vanishes due to the previous reasoning.
4. If the previous analysis does not immediately apply to your arm, your understanding is still on a coarser level.

17. Extending This Insight to What You Own

1. Internal phenomena, such as your mind and your body, belong to you and therefore are "yours."
2. External belongings, such as your clothing or car, also are "yours."
3. If the "I" does not inherently exist, what is "yours" could not possibly inherently exist.

18. BALANCING CALM AND INSIGHT

For the time being, alternate a little stabilizing meditation with a little analytical meditation in order both
to taste the process and to strengthen your current meditation.

1. First focus your mind on a single object, such as a Buddha image or your breath.
2. Use analytical meditation as described in the four
steps for meditating on the nature of the "I" (see
Chapter 15).
3. When you develop a little insight, stay with that insight in stabilizing meditation, appreciating its impact.
4. Then, when feeling diminishes a little, return to analytical meditation to reinstate feeling and develop
more insight.

Part V. How Persons and Things Actually Exist

19. VIEWING YOURSELF AS LIKE AN ILLUSION

1. Remember a time when you mistook a reflection of a
person in a mirror for an actual person.
2. It appeared to be a person but was not.
3. Similarly, all persons and things seem to exist from

their own side without depending on causes and conditions, on their parts, and on thought, but they do not.

4. In this way, persons and things are *like* illusions.

Then:

1. As you did earlier, bring the target of your reasoning, the inherently established "I," to mind by remembering or imagining an instance when you strongly believed in it.

2. Notice the ignorance that superimposes inherent existence, and identify it.

3. Put particular emphasis on contemplating the fact that if such inherent establishment exists, the "I" and the mind-body complex would have to be either the same or different.

4. Then forcefully contemplate the absurdity of assertions of the self and mind-body as either the same or different, seeing and feeling the impossibility of those assertions:

ONENESS

- "I" and mind-body would have to be utterly and in all ways one.

- In that case, asserting an "I" would be pointless.
- It would be impossible to think of "my body" or "my head" or "my mind."
- When mind and body no longer exist, the self also would not exist.
- Since mind and body are plural, a person's selves also would be plural.
- Since the "I" is just one, mind and body also would be one.
- Just as mind and body are produced and disintegrate, so it would have to be asserted that the "I" is inherently produced and inherently disintegrates. In this case, neither the pleasurable effects of virtuous actions nor the painful effects of nonvirtuous actions would bear fruit for us, or we would be experiencing the effects of actions we ourselves did not commit.

DIFFERENCE

- "I" and mind-body would have to be completely separate.
- In that case, the "I" would have to be findable after clearing away mind and body.

- The "I" would not have the characteristics of production, abiding, and disintegration, which is absurd.
- The "I" would absurdly have to be just a figment of the imagination or permanent.
- Absurdly, the "I" would not have any physical or mental characteristics.

5. Not finding such an "I," firmly decide, "Neither I nor any person is inherently established."

6. Remain for a while, absorbing the meaning of emptiness, concentrating on the absence of inherent establishment.

7. Then, once again let the appearances of people dawn to your mind.

8. Reflect on the fact that, within the context of dependent-arising, people also engage in actions and thus accumulate karma and experience the effects of those actions.

9. Ascertain the fact that the appearance of people is effective and feasible within the absence of inherent existence.

10. When effectiveness and emptiness seem to be contradictory, use the example of a mirror image:

- The image of a face is undeniably produced in dependence on a face and a mirror, even though it is empty of the eyes, ears, and so forth it appears to have, and the image of a face undeniably disappears when either face or mirror is absent.

- Similarly, although a person does not have even a speck of inherent establishment, it is not contradictory for a person to perform actions, accumulate karma, experience effects, and be born in dependence on karma and destructive emotions.

11. Try to view the lack of contradiction between effectiveness and emptiness with respect to all people and things.

20. NOTICING HOW EVERYTHING DEPENDS ON THOUGHT

1. Revisit a time when you were filled with hatred or desire.

2. Does it not seem that the hated or desired person or thing is extremely substantial, very concrete?

3. Since this is the case, there is no way you can claim that you already see phenomena as dependent on thought.

4. You see them as existing in their own right.

5. Remember that you need frequent meditation on emptiness to counter the false appearance of phenomena.

Then Consider:

1. The "I" is set up in dependence upon mind and body.

2. However, mind and body are not the "I," nor is the "I" mind and body.

3. Therefore, the "I" depends on conceptual thought, set up by the mind.

4. The fact that the "I" depends on thought implies that the "I" does not exist in and of itself.

5. Now notice that you have a better sense of what it means for something to exist in and of itself, the inherent existence that realization of emptiness is aimed at refuting.

Part VI. Deepening Love with Insight

21. FEELING EMPATHY

Apply these six similarities to yourself to understand the nature of your suffering and develop a strong intention to transcend this dynamic.

1. Just as a bucket in a well is bound by a rope, so I am constrained by counterproductive emotions and actions driven by them.

2. Just as the movement of a bucket up and down the well is run by an operator, so the process of my cyclic existence is run by my untamed mind, specifically through mistakenly believing that I inherently exist, and that "mine" inherently exists.

3. Just as a bucket travels up and down the well over and over, so I ceaselessly wander in the great well of cyclic existence, from the uppermost states of temporary happiness to the lowest states of temporary pain.

4. Just as it takes great exertion to draw the bucket up but it descends easily, so I have to expend great effort to draw myself upward to a happier life but easily descend to painful situations.

5. Just as a bucket does not determine its own movements, so the factors involved in shaping my life are the results of past ignorance, attachment, and grasping; in the present, these same factors are continually creating more problems for my future lives, like waves in the ocean.

6. Just as a bucket bumps against the walls of the well when it ascends and descends, so I am battered day by

day by the suffering of pain and change, and by being caught in processes beyond my control.

7. Therefore, from the depths of my heart I should seek to get out of this cyclic round of suffering.

Then:

Bring a friend to mind and think with feeling:

1. Just as a bucket in a well is bound by a rope, so this person is constrained by counterproductive emotions and actions driven by them.

2. Just as the movement of a bucket up and down the well is run by an operator, so the process of this person's cyclic existence is run by his or her untamed mind, specifically through mistakenly believing that he or she inherently exists, and that "mine" inherently exists.

3. Just as the bucket travels up and down the well over and over, so this person ceaselessly wanders in the great well of cyclic existence, from the uppermost states of temporary happiness to the lowest states of temporary pain.

4. Just as it takes great exertion to draw the bucket up but it descends easily, so this person has to expend great ef-

fort to rise upward to a happier life but easily descends to painful situations.

5. Just as a bucket does not determine its own movements, so the factors involved in shaping this person's life are the results of past ignorance, attachment, and grasping; in the present, these same factors are continually creating more problems for his or her future lives, like waves in the ocean.

6. Just as a bucket bumps against the walls of the well when it ascends and descends, so this person is battered day by day by the suffering of pain and change and by being caught in processes beyond his or her control.

Now cultivate three levels of love:

1. This person wants happiness but is bereft. How nice it would be if she or he could be imbued with happiness and all the causes of happiness!

2. This person wants happiness but is bereft. May she or he be imbued with happiness and all the causes of happiness!

3. This person wants happiness but is bereft. I will do

whatever I can to help her or him to be imbued with happiness and all the causes of happiness!

Now cultivate three levels of compassion:

1. This person wants happiness and does not want suffering, yet is stricken with terrible pain. If this person could only be free from suffering and the causes of suffering!

2. This person wants happiness and does not want suffering, yet is stricken with terrible pain. May this person be free from suffering and the causes of suffering!

3. This person wants happiness and does not want suffering, yet is stricken with terrible pain. I will help this person be free from suffering and all the causes of suffering!

Now cultivate total commitment:

1. Cyclic existence is a process driven by ignorance.

2. Therefore, it is realistic for me to work to achieve enlightenment and to help others do the same.

3. Even if I have to do it alone, I will free all sentient beings from suffering and the causes of suffering, and set all sentient beings in happiness and its causes.

One by one, bring to mind individual beings—first friends, then neutral persons, and then enemies, starting with the least offensive—and repeat these reflections with them.

22. REFLECTING ON IMPERMANENCE

Take this to heart:

1. It is certain that I will die. Death cannot be avoided. My life span is running out and cannot be extended.
2. When I will die is indefinite. Life spans among humans vary. The causes of death are many, and the causes of life comparatively few. The body is fragile.
3. At death nothing will help except my transformed attitude. Friends will be of no help. My wealth will be of no use, and neither will my body.
4. We are all in this same perilous situation, so there is no point in quarreling and fighting or wasting all our mental and physical energy on accumulating money and property.
5. I should practice now to reduce my attachment to passing fancies.
6. From the depths of my heart I should seek to get beyond this cycle of suffering induced by misconceiving the impermanent to be permanent.

Then consider:

1. My mind, body, possessions, and life are impermanent simply because they are produced by causes and conditions.

2. The very same causes that produce my mind, body, possessions, and life also make them disintegrate moment by moment.

3. The fact that things have a nature of impermanence indicates that they are not under their own power; they function under outside influence.

4. By mistaking what disintegrates moment by moment for something constant, I bring pain upon myself as well as others.

5. From the depths of my heart I should seek to get beyond this round of suffering induced by mistaking the impermanence for permanence.

Then:

Bring a friend to mind and consider the following with feeling:

1. This person's mind, body, possessions, and life are impermanent because they are produced by causes and conditions.

2. The very same causes that produce this person's mind, body, possessions, and life also make them disintegrate moment by moment.

3. The fact that things have a nature of impermanence indicates that they are not under their own power; they function under outside influence.

4. By mistaking what disintegrates moment by moment for something constant, this friend brings pain upon himself or herself as well as others.

Now cultivate three levels of love:

1. This person wants happiness but is bereft. How nice it would be if she or he could be imbued with happiness and all the causes of happiness!

2. This person wants happiness but is bereft. May she or he be imbued with happiness and all the causes of happiness!

3. This person wants happiness but is bereft. I will do whatever I can to help her or him to be imbued with happiness and all the causes of happiness!

Now cultivate three levels of compassion:

1. This person wants happiness and does not want suffering, yet is stricken with terrible pain. If this person

could only be free from suffering and the causes of suffering!

2. This person wants happiness and does not want suffering, yet is stricken with terrible pain. May this person be free from suffering and the causes of suffering!

3. This person wants happiness and does not want suffering, yet is stricken with terrible pain. I will help this person be free from suffering and all the causes of suffering!

Now cultivate total commitment:

1. Cyclic existence is a process driven by ignorance.

2. Therefore, it is realistic for me to work to achieve enlightenment and to help others do the same.

3. Even if I have to do it alone, I will free all sentient beings from suffering and the causes of suffering, and set all sentient beings in happiness and its causes.

One by one, bring to mind individual beings—first friends, then neutral persons, and then enemies, starting with the least offensive—and repeat these reflections with them.

23. ABSORBING YOURSELF IN ULTIMATE LOVE

1. As you did earlier, bring the target of your reasoning, the inherently established "I," to mind by remembering or imagining an instance when you strongly believed in it.

2. Notice the ignorance that superimposes inherent existence, and identify it.

3. Put particular emphasis on contemplating the fact that if such inherent establishment exists, the "I" and the mind-body complex would have to be either the same or different.

4. Then forcefully contemplate the absurdity of assertions of the self and mind-body as either the same or different, seeing and feeling the impossibility of those assertions:

ONENESS

- "I" and mind-body would have to be utterly and in all ways one.

- In that case, asserting an "I" would be pointless.

- It would be impossible to think of "my body," or "my head," or "my mind."

- When mind and body no longer exist, the self also would not exist.

- Since mind and body are plural, a person's selves also would be plural.

- Since the "I" is just one, mind and body also would be one.

- Just as mind and body are produced and disintegrate, so it would have to be asserted that the "I" is inherently produced and inherently disintegrates. In this case, neither the pleasurable effects of virtuous actions nor the painful effects of nonvirtuous actions would bear fruit for us, or we would be experiencing the effects of actions we ourselves did not commit.

DIFFERENCE

- "I" and mind-body would have to be completely separate.

- In that case, the "I" would have to be findable after clearing away mind and body.

- The "I" would not have the characteristics of production, abiding, and disintegration, which is absurd.

- The "I" would absurdly have to be just a figment of the imagination or permanent.

- Absurdly, the "I" would not have any physical or mental characteristics.

5. Not finding such an "I," firmly decide, "Neither I nor any person is inherently established."

6. Resolve: From the depths of my heart I should seek to get beyond this round of suffering brought on myself by misconceiving what does not inherently exist as inherently existing.

Then:

Bring a friend to mind and, while remembering the process of self-ruinous cyclic existence, consider the following:

1. Like me, this person is lost in an ocean of misapprehension of "I" as inherently existent, fed by a huge river of ignorance mistaking mind and body to be inherently existent, and agitated by winds of counterproductive thoughts and actions.

2. Like someone mistaking a reflection of the moon in water for the moon itself, this person mistakes the appearance of "I" and other phenomena to mean they exist in their own right.

3. By accepting this false appearance, this person is powerlessly drawn into lust and hatred, accumulating karma and being born over and over again in a round of pain.

4. Through this process this person unnecessarily brings pain upon himself or herself as well as others.

Now cultivate three levels of love:

1. This person wants happiness but is bereft. How nice it would be if she or he could be imbued with happiness and all the causes of happiness!

2. This person wants happiness but is bereft. May she or he be imbued with happiness and all the causes of happiness!

3. This person wants happiness but is bereft. I will do whatever I can to help her or him to be imbued with happiness and all the causes of happiness!

Now cultivate three levels of compassion:

1. This person wants happiness and does not want suffering, yet is stricken with terrible pain. If this person

could only be free from suffering and the causes of suffering!

2. This person wants happiness and does not want suffering, yet is stricken with terrible pain. May this person be free from suffering and the causes of suffering!

3. This person wants happiness and does not want suffering, yet is stricken with terrible pain. I will help this person be free from suffering and all the causes of suffering!

Now cultivate total commitment:

1. Cyclic existence is a process driven by ignorance.

2. Therefore, it is realistic for me to work to achieve enlightenment and to help others do the same.

3. Even if I have to do it alone, I will free all sentient beings from suffering and the causes of suffering, and set all sentient beings in happiness and its causes.

One by one, bring to mind individual sentient beings—first friends, then neutral persons, and then enemies, starting with the least offensive—and repeat these reflections with them.

Selected Readings

H. H. the Dalai Lama, Tenzin Gyatso. *How to Expand Love: Widening the Circle of Loving Relationships.* Translated and edited by Jeffrey Hopkins. New York: Atria Books/Simon & Schuster, 2005.

———. *How to Practice: The Way to a Meaningful Life.* Translated and edited by Jeffrey Hopkins. New York: Atria Books/Simon & Schuster, 2002.

———. *Kindness, Clarity, and Insight.* Translated and edited by Jeffrey Hopkins; coedited by Elizabeth Napper. Ithaca, N.Y.: Snow Lion Publications, 1984; rev. ed., 2006.

———. *The Meaning of Life: Buddhist Perspectives on Cause and Effect.* Translated and edited by Jeffrey Hopkins. Boston: Wisdom Publications, 2000.

———. *Mind of Clear Light: Advice on Living Well and Dying Consciously.* Translated and edited by Jeffrey Hopkins. New York: Atria Books/Simon & Schuster, 2002.

Hopkins, Jeffrey. *Buddhist Advice for Living and Liberation: Nagarjuna's Precious Garland.* Ithaca, N.Y.: Snow Lion Publications, 1998.

——. *Cultivating Compassion.* New York: Broadway Books, 2001.

——. *Emptiness Yoga.* Ithaca, N.Y.: Snow Lion Publications, 1987.

——. *Meditation on Emptiness.* London: Wisdom Publications, 1983; rev. ed., Boston: Wisdom Publications, 1996.

Rinchen, Geshe Sonam, and Ruth Sonam. *Yogic Deeds of Bodhisattvas: Gyel-tsap on Aryadeva's Four Hundred.* Ithaca, N.Y.: Snow Lion Publications, 1994.

Tsong-kha-pa. *The Great Treatise on the Stages of the Path to Enlightenment,* vols. 1–3. Translated and edited by Joshua W. C. Cutler and Guy Newland. Ithaca, N.Y.: Snow Lion Publications, 2000 and 2003.

Wallace, Vesna A., and B. Alan Wallace. *A Guide to the Bodhisattva Way of Life.* Ithaca, N.Y.: Snow Lion Publications, 1997.

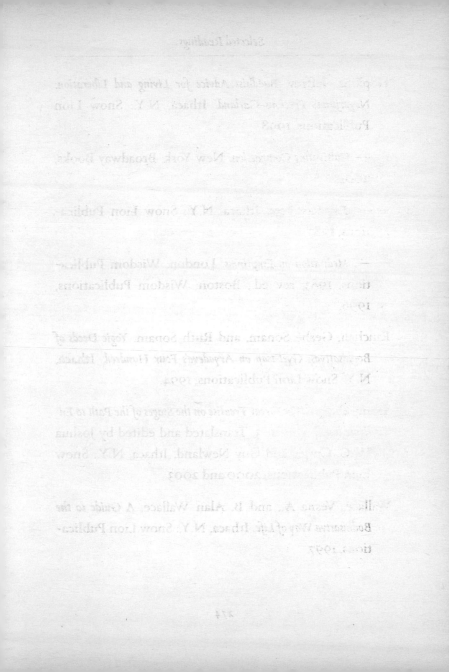

...pa. *Mirror of Wisdom: Advice for Living and Liberation.* Napper. Translated. Ithaca, N.Y. Snow Lion Publications, 2003

——. *Emptiness Yoga.* Ithaca, New York. Broadway Books ...

——. ... Ithaca, N.Y. Snow Lion Publications ...

——. *Meditation on Emptiness.* London. Wisdom Publications, 1983; rev. ed. Boston. Wisdom Publications, 1996

Kunsang, Gesh Sonam, and Ruth Sonam. *Yogic Deeds of Bodhisattvas: Gyel-tsen on Aryadeva's Four Hundred.* Ithaca, N.Y. Snow Lion Publications, 1994.

——. ... *Treatise on the Stages of the Path to En...* Translated and edited by Joshua W. C. Cutler and Guy Newland. Ithaca, N.Y. Snow Lion Publications, 2000 and 2002

Wallace, Vesna A., and B. Alan Wallace. *A Guide to the Bodhisattva Way of Life.* Ithaca, N.Y. Snow Lion Publications, 1997